ポケモン×工芸
美とわざの大発見

POKÉMON×KOGEI
Playful Encounters of Pokémon and Japanese Craft

ごあいさつ

「ポケモン」と「工芸」、ふだんあまり見ない単語の並びで意外に感じた方も多いかと思います。1996年に発売されたゲームソフト『ポケットモンスター 赤・緑』からはじまったポケモンは、今やだれもが知っている大人気コンテンツとして、国や地域、言語の壁を越えて、世界中の人々を魅了し続けています。ポケモンで遊んで育った子どもたちが大人になり、自身の子どもや孫と一緒にポケモンを楽しむなど、幅広い世代の心を結び付けるコンテンツでもあります。そんなポケモンが今回出会ったのが工芸です。

長い歴史のなかで、機能や装飾性をフル稼働して日々の生活を支えてきた工芸は、今日では自立した造形作品として展開しており、なかでも日本はその豊かさと多彩さとを誇ります。数々の作品に浮かび上がるのは作り手の素材への深い理解、高度な技術、そして熱い意志。同時に日本的な自然観や精神世界にも気づかされ、関心はますます高まります。

本展覧会では人間国宝から注目の若手まで、現代日本の工芸を代表する20名のアーティストが、ポケモンをテーマに工芸の多種多様な素材と技法で作品を制作しました。すべてがこの展覧会のための新作であり、そのひとつひとつから各アーティストによるポケモンへのさまざまな挑戦を見て取ることができます。今まで見たことのないポケモン、今まで見たことのない工芸作品。この展覧会でご鑑賞いただく皆様には、たくさんの新しい発見が訪れることと思います。

ぜひ、ポケモンと工芸の出会いに立会い、あなただけの大発見をお楽しみください。

最後になりましたが、本展を開催するにあたり、ご協力を賜りました関係者各位に心より御礼申し上げます。

主催者

Foreword

"POKÉMON × KOGEI": Many of you might be surprised to find these words together. Since the 1996 release of the video games *Pokémon Red and Pokémon Green*, Pokémon has evolved into an extremely popular and universally recognizable brand that continues to fascinate the entire world, transcending the geographical and language boundaries. It brings together a wide range of generations. Children who grew up playing the video game can enjoy it again with their own children and grandchildren. Now Pokémon meets *kogei*, or craft.

Throughout its long history, *kogei* supported our everyday life by putting their functionality and decorative qualities to full use. Today, *kogei* has evolved into an autonomous form of art, in whose richness and variety Japan takes particular pride. A deep understanding of materials, refined skills, and a passionate determination are evident in many pieces. At the same time, they offer an insight into Japan's unique view of nature and spirituality, further stimulating our interest.

For this exhibition, 20 leading artists of contemporary Japanese *kogei*, ranging from living national treasures to up-and-coming talents, have realized works on the theme of Pokémon in a wide variety of materials and techniques. All the objects have been created exclusively for this occasion, each demonstrating the various approaches each artist took to the subject. Pokémon and *kogei* as you have never seen them before: the show will offer many new revelations.

We invite you to witness the encounter between Pokémon and *kogei* and enjoy your own great discoveries.

Last but not least, we would like to express our sincere gratitude to all those involved for their generous support in organizing this exhibition.

Organizers

展覧会に寄せて

ポケモンと工芸が出会うと何が起こるだろう──そんな期待に胸をワクワクさせながら東京国立近代美術館工芸館（現・国立工芸館）を訪ねたのは、2019年秋のことでした。日本の工芸は、何世代にもわたって受け継がれた美意識や技を今に伝えると共に、時代性や作家の探究心によって「進化」しています。ポケモンというテーマをぶつけることで、作家の心に火をつけたいという思いと、アートとのかけ算による豊かなポケモン体験を、多くの方に楽しんでいただきたいという思いがそこにはありました。3年半の月日を経て、こうして現代日本を代表する20名のアーティストによる、ポケモンとの「真剣勝負」を皆様にご披露できるのは、とてもうれしい出来事です。

作家の中には「ポケモンを遊びながら育った」という方も、「ポケモンは初めて」という方もいらっしゃいましたが、久しぶりに、あるいはご家族や教え子の助けを借りながら新作ゲームをプレイし、「ポケモンずかん」と睨めっこしながら、理解や愛着を深めていただきました。それが創作へのモチベーションに変わった瞬間、一気にペースが上がります。アイデアが湧き、スケッチ、ディスカッション、試作を繰り返しながら、作品づくりが進んでいったのです。陶芸、漆芸、木工、金工、染織……工芸とひとくちに言っても、素材や技法は多様で、作家のアプローチや表現もユニークです。20名のアーティストがポケモンにどのように向き合い、どのような美とわざをしかけてきたのか、ぜひ見て、感じてください。

株式会社ポケモン

For the Exhibition “POKÉMON × KOGEI”

What would happen when Pokémon meets *kogei* (craft)? It was with such anticipation and excitement that we visited Crafts Gallery, the National Museum of Modern Art, Tokyo (now the National Crafts Museum) in the fall of 2019. *Kogei* in Japan has evolved—just like Pokémon—with the times and artists' explorations, while continuing the aesthetics and skills passed down over generations. Calling on the artists to take on Pokémon, we wanted to ignite their creativity. It was also our hope that the chemistry between art and Pokémon would generate a rich experience that many people might enjoy. After three and a half years, it is our great pleasure to present “epic battles” with Pokémon, brought to life by 20 of Japan's leading contemporary artists.

Some of the artists grew up playing Pokémon, while others were new to its world. For the first time in a while—some with the help of their families and students—they played the latest video games and developed their understanding and love of Pokémon by poring over the *Pokédex*. The moment this turned into creative motivation, the pace quickly picked up. Ideas began to bubble up, and through repeated sketches, discussions, and prototyping, artwork production proceeded. Ceramics, lacquerwork, woodwork, metalwork, dyeing, weaving...*Kogei* includes a wide variety of materials and techniques, and each artist has a unique approach and expression. We invite you to look and feel how the 20 artists interpreted Pokémon and experience the beauty and skill they applied to it.

The Pokémon Company

目次
Contents

ポケモンと工芸の出会いが生むインパクト

唐澤昌宏（国立工芸館長）

スマートフォン用アプリ「ポケモンGO」が日本でサービスを開始した2016年7月22日を、いまでもはっきりと覚えている。それまではゲーム機で遊んでいる子どもたちを横目で見ていたが、あらためて「ポケモン」という言葉の響きに興味をいだき、何もわからないままスマートフォンにアプリをインストールした。下調べをしなかったこともあり、遊び方は手探りで、はじめはポケストップ（フィールドマップにある青いモニュメント）を回してアイテムを入手することさえもわからなかった。その後も短時間ではあったが、何気なくアプリを立ち上げてはコツコツと楽しんできた。

そのような中、株式会社ポケモンさんから「工芸とポケモンとのコラボレーションで、本格的な展覧会を開催したいのですが」と話をいただいた。その時、正直なところ何も思いつかなかった。が、なぜか「とても興味があります、考えてみたいですね」とだけ答えた。東京国立近代美術館工芸館（現・国立工芸館）が東京・北の丸から石川・金沢への移転に向けて準備をしていたこともあり、それくらいの返事しかできなかったのだ。ただその後も、ポケモンさんから熱き想いを何度もいただき、多種多様なポケモンと、同じく多彩な工芸の世界が繋がると、とても楽しい新たな世界が広がるのではと考えるようになり、徐々に展覧会の計画が具体化していった。

「ポケモンと工芸を結び付けて何ができるだろうか」。真っ先に頭に浮かんだのが、ポケモンはいまやゲームやアニメなどを通して世界中で知られているということ。それを入り口にして「世代を超えて多彩な工芸の素晴らしさを、より広く知ってもらえる」「日本発信のポケモンなら、日本の工芸の奥深さを伝えるに相応しい」かもしれないと、何の根拠もなかったが、工芸側の視点から二つの出会いによる相乗的な効果に期待が膨らんだ。

日本の工芸の奥深さの一つとして、さまざまな素材からつくり出される質感を、つくり手それぞれが引き出し、それを表現と一体化させて見せているところがある。そのことを工芸素材によるポケモン制作に当てはめると、液晶画面からでは感じ取れない独特で固有の表情を持つポケモンたちが、私たちの目の前に現れることになる。それも三次元で、かつ質感がともなったポケモンたちだ。想像するだけでワクワク感がとまらない。

ポケモンと工芸が出会ったことで生み出される作品世界は、二つの文化を繋ぐだけでなく、まったく新しい価値観や豊かさを感じさせずにはいられない。世代に関係なく、是非、多くの方に観て楽しんでいただきたいと思う。それだけの感動と刺激を与えてくれるに違いない。

The Powerful Encounter between Pokémon and *Kogei*

Karasawa Masahiro (Director, the National Crafts Museum)

I still clearly remember July 22, 2016, when the smartphone app "Pokémon GO" was launched in Japan. I had seen children playing with video game consoles, but on that day the word "Pokémon" caught my imagination, and I installed the app on my smartphone without knowing what to expect. I did not do my homework, and at first I did not even know that I had to turn PokéStops (blue monuments on the field map) in order to pick up items. Since then, I have continued to casually launch the app, enjoying it piecemeal.

In the meantime, The Pokémon Company approached me with the idea of holding a full-scale exhibition combining *kogei* with Pokémon. At the time, I honestly did not know what to make of it. Without knowing why, though, I found myself replying that I was very interested and would like to give it some thought. That was about all I could say, as Crafts Gallery, the National Museum of Modern Art, Tokyo (now the National Crafts Museum) was preparing to relocate from Kitanomaru, Tokyo, to Kanazawa, Ishikawa. However, the company never tired of expressing their enthusiasm afterwards, and I began to think that connecting the diverse universe of Pokémon with the equally varied world of *kogei* might open up an exciting new horizon. The exhibition plan gradually began to take shape.

What can we do by connecting Pokémon and *kogei*? The first thing that came to my mind was Pokémon's global recognition through its video game and anime franchises. A genuine made-in-Japan product, Pokémon would be an ideal vehicle for broadcasting the depth of Japanese craftspersonship to a wider audience. Although it was still nothing concrete at the time, from *kogei*'s perspective I was excited about the synergistic effect that the meeting of the two would produce.

One indication of the Japanese *kogei*'s depth is in the way each craftsperson draws out the textures from various materials, making them part and parcel of his/her own mode of expression. When this is applied to Pokémon produced with *kogei* materials, the familiar creatures emerge with a unique and distinctive expressiveness that they never had on the screen. Pokémon in three dimensions and with texture: the thought of it alone fills our hearts with excitement.

The world created by the meeting of Pokémon and *kogei* not only connects two very different cultures but also evokes compelling, entirely new values and richness. I hope that many people, regardless of generation, will see and enjoy this exhibition. It is sure to provide emotion and stimulation.

- 本書は「ポケモン×工芸展――美とわざの大発見」の公式図録として刊行した。
- 解説は今井陽子（国立工芸館）が執筆した。
- This book was published in conjunction with *POKÉMON x KOGEI—Playful Encounters of Pokémon and Japanese Craft*, an exhibition organized by the National Crafts Museum.
- Artists' descriptions were written by Imai Yoko (National Crafts Museum).

Appearance — Approach!

1 すがた——迫る！

工芸の技がポケモンを思いがけない物質のなかから呼び起こしました。それぞれの作家が日頃から向き合ってきた金属、土、木などの素材研究、そして長年の鍛錬による優れた技術の成果が、ポケモンのフォルムはもちろん、皮膚や毛並み、仕草や表情に抽出され、また気配や出現の瞬間をもみごとに捉えています。それらを描写する要素はすべて、作家たちが工芸に発見したきらめきばかり。そのせいか、ここに生息するどのポケモンも迫力に満ち、なんだかとても新鮮です。五感を研ぎ澄まし、ポケモンたちとの出会いを満喫してください。

●

Eyes and motions for craft have evoked Pokémon from unexpected materials. The artists' research of materials such as metal, clay, and wood, which they have been dealing with day in and day out, and their excellent techniques developed over many years of forging, are extracted not only in the form of Pokémon, but also in its skin, fur, gesture, and expression, and they also beautifully capture signs and moments of appearance. All elements depicted here are sparkles that the artists have discovered in their craft. Perhaps that is why every Pokémon in this exhibition is so powerful and fresh. We hope you will sharpen your senses and enjoy your encounter with Pokémon to the fullest.

吉田泰一郎　Yoshida Taiichiro

ブースター | Flareon

[左]イーブイ｜[left] Eevee
[右]サンダース｜[right] Jolteon

金工
Metal Works

吉田泰一郎

Yoshida Taiichiro

[上]《サンダース》に用いる鏨 | 《サンダース》のパーツは、日本では豊作の象徴である雷のイメージ。サンダースをはじめイーブイ進化形の3匹のパーツには、ポケモンたちの属性と日本の伝統意匠を重ね、「工芸」というきわめて日本的なものの在り方への道筋を開いた。
[下]《イーブイ》に吉田が見た性格は「ノーマル」で、そこにあらゆる可能性を期待した。鏨にはイーブイの進化形として確認されている8種のポケモンのタイプに加え、その他のタイプもシンボリックに表現。お気に入りのポケモンを連想させる形を発見するのもまた楽しい。
[top] Chisels used to make *Jolteon*. | Jolteon's parts are the image of thunderstorms. In Japan, thunderstorms symbolize a good harvest. Eevee's three Evolutions, including Jolteon, combine the attributes of Pokémon and traditional Japanese design, paving the way for a very Japanese mode of craft.
[bottom] Yoshida sees *Eevee*'s personality as "normal," and he expected various possibilities to emerge from it. In addition to the eight Pokémon attributes that have been identified as Evolutions of Eevee, other types are also symbolically represented on these chisels he devised. Enjoy discovering shapes that remind you of your favorite Pokémon.

•

外側

吉田泰一郎が挑んだのは**イーブイ**とその進化形3匹。なぜイーブイ?「やはり『ポケットモンスター 赤・緑』に登場したポケモンが思い出深い。なかでもイーブイは、当時は入手方法が独特で、人からもらうしかなかった」。そしてさまざまに進化する点が、吉田が扱う銅とリンクすることも見逃せません。

今回もイーブイでは純銅の色艶がフル稼働。さらに化学変化を駆使して**シャワーズ**には青銅、**サンダース**は金銀メッキ、**ブースター**のためには緋銅という銅の伝統着色を施しました。耳などに用いた黒色も銅の硫化によります。パーツの成形に用いたのは、抜き鏨(たがね)をヒントに吉田が独自に考案したスペシャル版。クッキー型のように金属板に押し当てると、切り抜きながら文様を表わせるものです。すべて自作。大学院で「鏨仕事は道具作りが8割」と開眼して以降、造形言語の最小単位にして最大の効果を発揮する要素と捉えています。

準備が整ったらスチレンフォームにパーツを次々と差し、スケッチや粘土で段階的に作り上げてきた全体像を呼び起こします。このプロセスで大切にしているのは「リズム」。大小を使い分け、粗密と陰影、そして何より「カッコイイ」ことを見定めながら進めていきます。

•

内側

吉田がふだんの仕事で取り上げるモチーフは動物です。リアルサイズなので、今回のイーブイ進化形たちのような迫力を示すこともしばしばで、「こんな風に動物をドーンと作る感覚は、結構ポケモンの影響がでかい」のだとか。もっとも、それは彫金の伝統から装飾性だけを抽出して純然たる造形を目指した結果であって、そこに物語の要素を持ち込むことはしませんでした。

しかし今回はポケモンが題材です。タイプに加えて、いろいろな物語がポケモンにはあります。そこで吉田は資料を検証しながら、選んだ4匹の内面性を考えるという試みに挑戦し、さりげない佇まいにも意味を忍ばせました。こんなに大きな眼球もやはり初めてだったという七宝焼のガラス質に潤んだ光が宿り、内なる想いに触れる喜びをもたらします。

イーブイ
Eevee

シャワーズ
Vaporeon

サンダース
Jolteon

ブースター
Flareon

Exterior

Yoshida Taiichiro took on the challenge of creating **Eevee** and its original three Evolutions. Why Eevee? "*Pokémon Red and Pokémon Green* are memorable to me. At the time there was a unique way of acquiring this particular Eevee—we had no choice but to get it from other people." It is also important to note that the various Evolutions of Eevee connect to the copper that is Yoshida's material.

Here, the color and gloss of pure copper is showcased to the fullest in Eevee. Further chemical changes were used to produce bronze for **Vaporeon**, gold and silver gilting for **Jolteon**, and a traditional scarlet patina called *hido* for **Flareon**. The black used for the ears and other parts is also due to the sulfurization of copper. The chisel used to shape the parts is a special version that Yoshida devised himself, inspired by a traditional *nukitagane* (punching chisel). When it is pressed against metal plate like a cookie-cutter, designs can be rendered while being cut out. He makes all his chisels himself. Since realizing in graduate school that "80% of chisel work is making tools," he considers it the smallest yet most effective element of his modeling vocabulary.

When ready, he inserts parts one after another into styrene foam and calls the overall image into being step by step with sketches and clay. What is important in this process is "rhythm": he alternates between large and small, coarse and fine, shadow and highlight, and above all makes sure as he proceeds that "it's cool to look at."

Interior

Yoshida's usual subjects are animals. Because they are actual size, they often appear as powerful as the evolved forms of Eevee featured here. He says, "The feeling of creating a large animal like this is greatly influenced by Pokémon." This is the result of extracting only the decorative qualities from the tradition of metal carving and aiming for purely figurative forms, and he has never introduced any narrative elements.

This time, however, the subject is Pokémon, and in addition to their types, Pokémon are accompanied by various stories. Yoshida therefore took on the challenge of examining the material and thinking about the internal nature of the four Pokémon he chose, noting that even their casual appearances conceal hidden meanings. The glass cloisonné, which he used to create the largest eyeballs he has ever made, is infused with fluid light, delivering the joy of engaging with the creatures' inner thoughts.

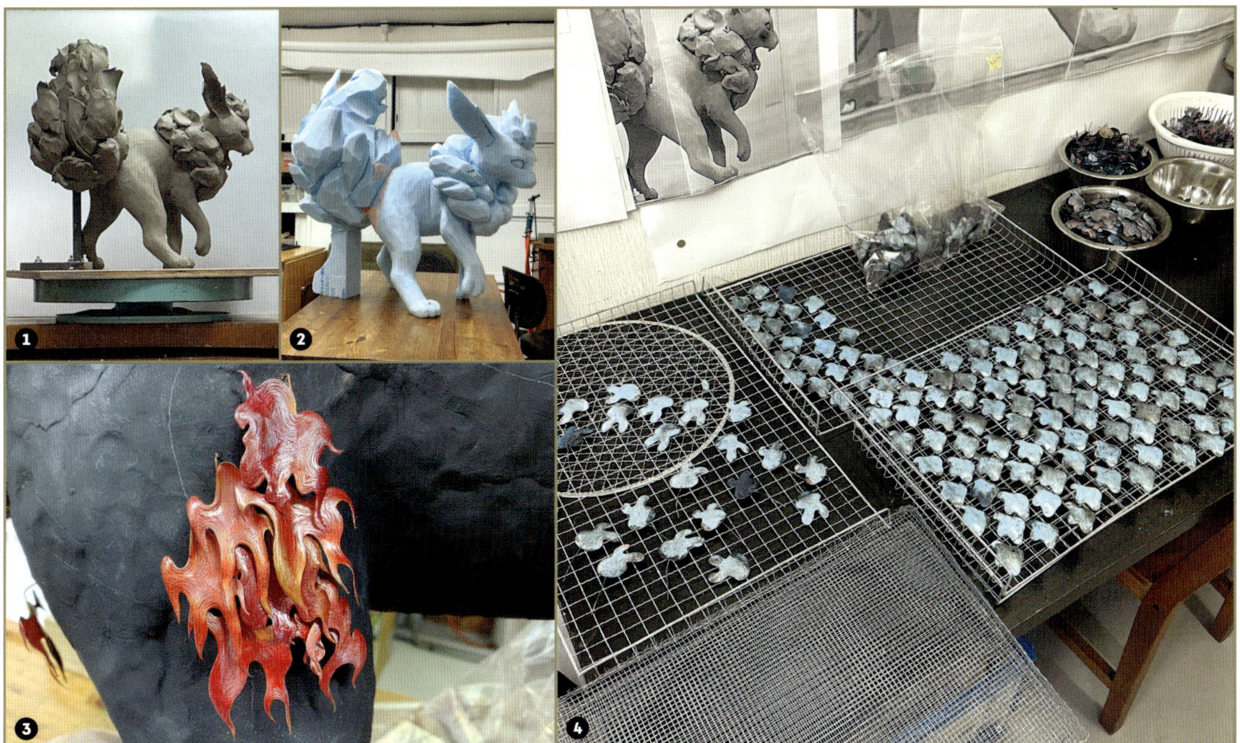

❶《ブースター》の制作｜粘土で作ったマケットを撮影し、サイズ感を確認。
❷《ブースター》｜スチレンフォームを削り出していく。
❸《ブースター》｜スチレンフォームにエポキシ樹脂を塗り、火焔パーツを差し込んでいく。
❹《シャワーズ》パーツ｜流水文を緑青で彩色し、水感をアップ。

❶ *Flareon* in progress | A clay maquette is photographed to verify its sense of scale.
❷ *Flareon* | Carving forms from styrene foam.
❸ *Flareon* | Epoxy resin is applied to styrene foam, and flame parts are inserted.
❹ Parts for *Vaporeon* | The flowing water pattern is tinted greenish blue to enhance the sense of the aquatic.

満田晴穂　Mitsuta Haruo

自在トランセル・バタフリー | Articulated Metapod/Butterfree

自在コクーン・スピアー | Articulated Kakuna/Beedrill

満田晴穂
Mitsuta Haruo

自在置物

金属を素材とする置物で、モチーフは動物。高度な写実性に加え、実物同様に各パーツを自由に動かせるのが特徴です。鑑賞性とともに複雑な構造の妙を味わえるこのオブジェクトは、江戸時代、太平の世が続き仕事が減少した甲冑師が始め、いわゆる「超絶技巧」を志向した明治の工芸ブームのなかで最盛期を迎えました。海外でも高く評価されたものの、しかし工芸の主流が変わると衰微。満田晴穂は、現代においてこの稀少な技術を継承する自在置物の第一人者です。

制作はまずは対象とする昆虫などの身体を生物学的に理解するところから始まります。それを自在置物の分節に置換。「なぜその形なのか。そこには生きるための理由がある。環境や生態系との関係を知る。制作するうちにわかるそうしたことに惹かれる」。可動する仕掛けの正解は生きもののなかに求められますが、それを物理的に実現するのはしばしば挑戦となります。「カチッと嵌まったときがまた面白い」。

アトリエ | 標本や書籍、過去の作品と並ぶバタフリーたち。「取材を始めて1年。制作にかかってから3、4ヵ月経つともう"いるもの"になる。不思議なものでリアリティを帯びてくる」。
Studio | Specimens, books, past works, and Butterfree and other Pokémon pieces lined up together. "It took a year from which I started gathering information. After three or four months spent producing them, I got to the 'They're here' stage. It's a strange feeling, filled with reality."

思いをめぐらせる

今回満田が選んだモチーフは、むしタイプや**ギャラドス**など。いずれも子どもの頃、ゲームで仲間にしていたポケモンたちです。通常のプロセスではスケッチの次は採寸と解剖に進みますが、ポケモンは私たちの現実とは異なる世界線の生きものです。満田が自身の仕事で重視しているのは「いかに自分を出さないか」「忠実に対象を写し取るか」ということですが、ポケモンをモチーフとする制作では、"正解"を目の前に置いた答え合わせができません。「とはいえポケモンが存在するという世界はさまざまな媒体で構築されている。そこに思いをめぐらせることはできる」。蜂や蝶などの文脈からもフォルムの必然を探り、同時にふだんはしない判断、すなわち自分を出す行為を重ねて、印象と工芸の論理のあいだで「ちょうどいいところを攻めて」いきました。

そうするうちに、自在置物の伝統にある龍や鯱(しゃち)（姿は魚で虎の頭をもつとされる幻獣）に挑んだ昔の人も同様だったのかもしれないと、時間を超えて思いが広がります。「資料を集め、いろいろな解釈や表現を自分のなかに取り込み、再構築して立体物を作り出したに違いない。この感覚かと感動した」。ギャラドスは、みず・ひこうタイプであり、ドラゴンタイプではないがと断りながら、今回「自在置物として、満田の龍としてギャラドス」も制作しました。髭は迷った結果、可動節によって垂れ下がるのはカッコよくないと判断。「そういえば昔の龍の髭も動かない」。制作を通して、過去と満田の視点がここでも重なります。

Articulated Figurines

Articulated metal figurines have animals as their theme. In addition to being highly realistic, they are distinctive in that their parts can be moved freely, just like actual animals' bodies. Such objects, which prepare their exquisite mechanism along with appreciative qualities, were initiated by armorers, whose work shrank during the Great Peace of the Edo period, and reached their peak during the craft boom of the Meiji era, in which the goal was transcendent technical skills. While they were also highly regarded overseas, as

トランセル
Metapod

バタフリー
Butterfree

コクーン
Kakuna

スピアー
Beedrill

ギャラドス
Gyarados

trends in the craft changed, they fell into a decline. Mitsuta Haruo is the leading articulated figurine artist carrying on that extremely rare technique today.

His work begins by analyzing, biologically, the insect or other creature that is his subject. Then he translates his understanding of its body into the parts that will make up an articulated figurine. "Why is it shaped like this? There is a reason related to its existence, how it lives, behind it. I learn about its relationship to its environment and ecology. I am fascinated by understanding such things in the process of creating my work." The right answer to what the moveable component is found within the creature itself, but bringing that off in an object, physically, is challenging. "When it clicks perfectly, that's fun."

•

Pondering

The subjects Mitsuta chose for this project are Bug-type Pokémon and **Gyarados**, etc. These are Pokémon that he associated with in the video games, as a child. His usual process would be to follow sketching by measuring and dissecting the creature he has chosen, but Pokémon live on a different world from our reality. Mitsuta focuses in his work on "How I don't express myself?" and "Am I copying my subject accurately?", but with Pokémon as his subject, he cannot check his work against a correct answer before him. "But the world Pokémon inhabit is constructed of various media. I can ponder them there." He searches for the necessary forms in terms of the contexts of the bee or butterfly, for example, while at the same time makes decisions he does not usually consider, which allow him to express himself. In between his impression of the subject and the logic of his craft, he "goes after the perfect balance."

His thoughts broaden to cross to other times, wondering if the craftsmen of the past who tackled subjects such as dragons and *shachi* (a mythical animal with the head of a lion and the body of a fish), which are part of the articulated figurine tradition, did it the same way. "They undoubtedly collected reference materials, immersed themselves in all sorts of interpretations and styles, reconstructed with the results, and created three-dimensional figures. Was it this kind of sensation? I felt moved by the connection." While explaining that Gyarados is a Water- and Flying-type Pokémon, not Dragon-type, he created "Gyarados, as an articulated figurine, as a Mitsuta dragon." The whiskers were a problem, but he concluded that it wouldn't have been cool to have them dangling down from a moveable joint. "Actually, in the past, dragons' whiskers did not move." Through his creative process, past and present, Mitsuta's point of view, overlapped.

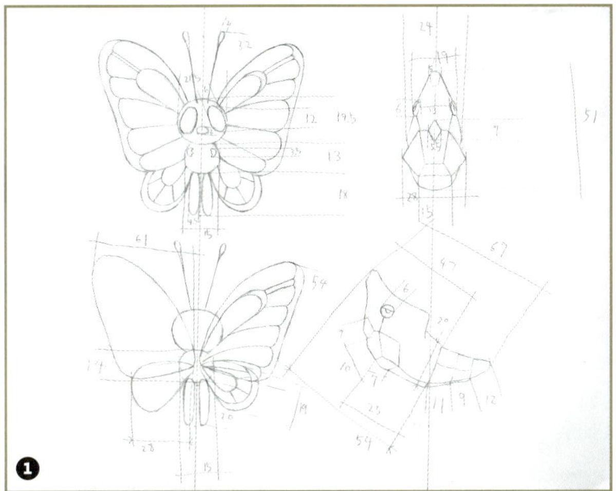

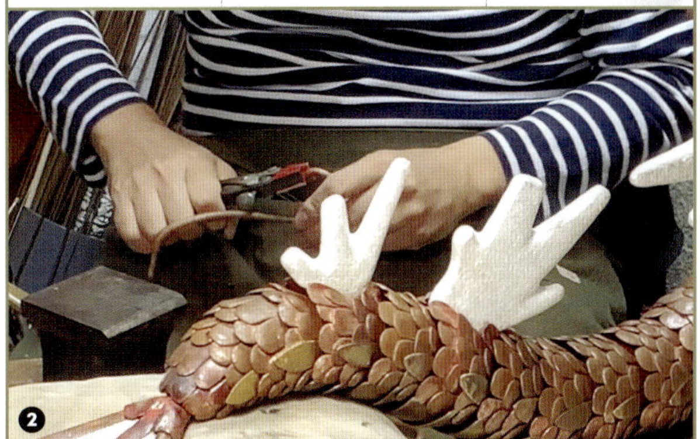

❶《自在トランセル・バタフリー》エスキース
❷《自在ギャラドス》(制作中) | 髭のカーブを微調整。付けて確認し、外して左右差を比べ、「気持ちいいバランス」を探りながらまた調整…を延々と繰り返す。「もともとが銅の棒。金属の硬さをどうなくすか」。生きものらしさを詰める、一番好きな時間。
❸《自在コクーン・スピアー》(部分) | パーツごとの動きは非常になめらか。脚先は附節を設けて細かく動かせる。「ゲームで脚先が動いているのを見て『よし!』と思った。昆虫としては動いてほしかったから。

❶ Sketch, *Articulated Metapod/Butterfree*
❷ *Articulated Gyarados* (in process) | Subtly adjusting the curve of its whisker. Attach it, check, remove it, compare left and right: in seeking "a good balance," the steps went on and on. "Originally, they were copper rods. How to eliminate the metal's stiffness?" Packing the work with lifelike qualities was the part of the process he liked best.
❸ *Articulated Kakuna/Beedrill* (partial) | Each of the parts moved extremely smoothly. Providing a tarsus on each of the feet let them move delicately. "Seeing the feet moving in the game, I thought, 'I figured!' I wanted it to move like an insect."

福田亨　Fukuda Toru

雨あがり | After Rain

木工
Wood Works

福田亨

Fukuda Toru

•

木象嵌

象嵌は文字通り、象(かたど)り、嵌(は)める技法。福田亨が木象嵌を始めたのは美術工芸高校に在学中のこと。木材の多彩な色が絵画にも使えそうだと考えたのがきっかけでしたが、ボディとなる木を彫って、そこに別の木をぴたりと嵌めていく「その繰り返し、パズルのような作業がしっくりときた」のだそうです。京都で伝統の指物技法を修得後、20歳頃から本格的に木象嵌を主体とする制作に取りかかりました。

《飛昇》部分｜ホウオウの各部を組み合わせる。釘を使わない指物の技。
Flying, detail | Assembling the various parts of Ho-Oh, using the *sashimono* technique of nail-free joinery.

一般には平面構成で行うこの技法を、福田は立体造形として展開。《雨あがり》の**アゲハント**でも、羽根の模様パーツを嵌める位置に合わせてそれぞれ微妙に異なる曲面として彫り出し、繊細な薄さのなかにしなやかな生命感を吹き込みました。現在福田が所持している素材は木の種類で160ほど。木目や節の入り方や使う向き、またそれらの順列組合せによって色調の幅は数倍にも広がります。「だから木っ端もなかなか捨てられない」。

•

「自然美」

福田が自然美を見る場は人間の居住地からほど近く。「原生林や大平原といったところではなく、人の営みとの関わりのなかに入り込んできた様子」に惹かれるのだといいます。切り取って愛でるその眼差しはとても日本的。そして「昆虫などを見てあれこれいう内容は、工芸で考えることと似ている」というのも興味深い指摘です。

今回の作品は自然と人工とがないまぜとなったところに立つ福田の芸術観に、ポケモンという別の世界線を重ねて構成されました。登場するポケモンは、福田が子どもの頃夢中になった『ポケットモンスター サファイア』などからの3匹。アゲハントは雨上がりの土から吸水中の図。「こんな風に蝶が水を吸うのはオスだけ」なので、アゲハントもきっとそうだろうと想像を膨らませ、オス仕様としました。**アリアドス**のステージは畳敷きです。見事な畳目感は、ミズナラの柾目の繊維に対して直角に彫り出して表現。「人間の匂いがする意匠」を意識し、石川県我谷村（現・加賀市）の民具から引用しました。現実界の蜘蛛は「怖い」という福田。蜘蛛を思わせる容姿をもつアリアドスですが、どこか愛らしい雰囲気もあり、どう見るかは鑑賞者の想像に委ねられました。一番好きだったというホウオウは、どこまでも高く飛翔する姿への憧れを螺旋形に組んだタワーで表象。子どもの成長を願う麻の葉文様を構造に採用し、ホウオウの飛来で虹がかかるという伝説を重ねて、吉祥の気分を高めました。

•

指物(さしもの)：金釘を用いず、木材に凹凸を彫ってはめ込む枘(ほぞ)差しなどで組み合わせて作られたもの、またその技法。板材を接合することにより、箱ものや机、箪笥(たんす)など、用途に合わせた形状と丈夫で複雑な構造が可能となる。

アリアドス
Ariados

ホウオウ
Ho-Oh

アゲハント
Beautifly

Inlaid Woodwork

Inlaid woodwork (*mokuzogan*) involves hand-cutting wood and inlaying it. Fukuda Toru began working with the technique when he was a student at an arts and crafts high school. It seemed to him that the variously colored pieces of wood could also be used for paintings, and he "felt comfortable with the repetitive, puzzle-like process" of carving a piece of wood for the body and then fitting other pieces of wood into it. After learning traditional *sashimono* techniques in Kyoto, he began practicing inlaid woodwork in earnest around the age of 20.

While this technique is generally used for two-dimensional compositions, Fukuda has developed it as a three-dimensional art form. In *After Rain*, the parts patterned with wings on **Beautifly** are carved with slightly different curvatures according to the position where they are to be fitted, infusing the thin and delicate piece with a supple sense of vitality. Fukuda currently has about 160 different types of wood in his possession. By varying the grain, knots, direction of placement and order of assembly, the range of color tones can be expanded several times over. "That's why I can never throw away even a scrap of wood."

"The Beauty of Nature"

The places Fukuda goes to observe the beauty of nature are close to people's residences. He says he is drawn "not so much to primeval forests or great plains as to place where nature intertwines with human activities. There is something very Japanese about the way he identifies and admires things in nature. Also, interestingly, he notes that "What I say when I look at insects is similar to what we think about craft."

Here, Fukuda's creative vision, at the intersection of nature and artifice, is superimposed on another world, that of Pokémon. The three Pokémon in these works are from the video game *Pokémon Sapphire*, which Fukuda loved as a child. Beautifly is drinking water from the soil after rain. Since "only male butterflies suck water like this," he imagined that Beautifly must be male, and gave him the appropriate characteristics. **Ariados** is on a stage covered with *tatami* mats. The marvelous texture of the mats is rendered by carving at right angles to straight grain fibers of *mizunara* oak. The design references the *wagatabon*, a folk tray from the village of Wagatani, Ishikawa Prefecture (present-day Kaga City), with the concept of "design that has a human source." Fukuda says he is "afraid of spiders" in the real world. While Ariados has a spider-like appearance, it also has an undeniable charm, and how to see it is left up to the viewer's imagination. The depiction of **Ho-Oh**, which he says was his favorite, represents longing to soar into the sky with a spiral tower. The tower is decorated with a hemp-leaf pattern imbued with prayers for the healthy growth of children, and a connection with the legend that a rainbow may appear when Ho-Oh flies over heightens the auspicious mood.

Sashimono: Woodwork done by carving convex and concave sections into wood and joining it without using metal hardware, and the technique used for this. By joining boards with this technique, it is possible to make boxes, desks, and chests of drawers of varying shape, sturdiness, and complexity to suit intended use.

1

2

3

❶《Floor》部分①｜アリアドスの住処を彫る。実際の畳目の凹凸と逆転した錯視的な効果に注目したい。
❷《Floor》部分②｜畳縁は寄木の手法で。薄く切り出した板を立てた状態で接合する。
❸《雨あがり》部分｜細かい彫り跡の陰影が雨に濡れた土の表面を想起させる。

❶ *Floor*, detail ① | Carving Ariados's dwelling. Note the illusory effect of reversal of the convex and concave of actual *tatami* mats.
❷ *Floor*, detaill ② | *Tatami* mat borders are made using the *yosegi* technique, with thinly sliced wood pieces joined in an upright position.
❸ *After Rain*, detail | Shadows of fine carved marks evoke the surface of rain-soaked soil.

今井完眞　Imai Sadamasa

［左］コイキング｜［left］Magikarp
［右］ゼニガメ｜［right］Squirtle

陶磁
Ceramics

今井完眞
Imai Sadamasa

「らしさ」

3代続く陶芸家の家に生まれた今井完眞。粘土を渡され、仕事場の片隅で遊んでいた幼年期を経て、早い時期から陶芸でやっていこうと決めました。生きものをモチーフとしたのも、土の感触や釉薬の照り艶に共通項を見いだしたからでした。でも生きもの、とくに変温動物が好きだったのも事実。カエル、蛇、トカゲ、亀、グリーンイグアナ、タコなどを飼い、今も「何か」がいる生活を送っています。

生きものと陶、それぞれの要素を探究した結果、今井の作風に対しては「写実的」という言葉がよく用いられます。が、今井にとってそれは「自分のキーワードではない。モチーフがもっている“らしさ”を表現する」のが主眼です。「計測や型取りをして作っても絶対に精気がない。極端にいえば、全然違う形を作って○○にしか見えないといわれるのが理想」。今井がモチーフから抽出したエッセンスを構築する。それが誰かの記憶の断片を手繰り寄せ、繋ぎ合わせて“実感”させる。作品を介してイメージの交感が起こり、発見の驚きと楽しさをもたらします。

プラスする

今井の制作は、手びねりボディを削りで攻めて、そして足して決めるスタイル。「土をつけるプラスの作業」で対象について考えていることを明らかにしていきます。

今回、《フシギバナ》の口元の細密な作り込みを今井はかなり楽しんだ様子。私たちも作品の隅々を眺めるうちに皮膚の凹凸に漂う陰影にまでも圧倒されそう。花の香りに誘われ向かった先でこのフシギバナと遭遇したら…。重厚な佇まいを前にして、自分だけの物語に胸が高鳴ります。

また、釉掛けもモデリングのうちと考えている今井。玉薬だけを使ったアーボックは、上絵だけで5回焼成を繰り返しました。「同じ上絵をベタ塗りして1回焼くとオモチャっぽくなることが多い。その上に釉を重ねたり、加筆して数回焼くと、だんだんと深みが出てくる」。

キングラーが乗っているのは漁具の1種の浮き玉です。「人工物と自然物の相性がすごくいい。組み合わせるのは海に落ちていそうなもの」。蟹を思わせるはさみポケモンのキングラーには

[左]《フシギバナ》の成形 | 粘土だけでもこれだけの迫力! たとえば球体の眼球を覆うまぶたはどうかかるのか。口元、耳の奥などはどこまで追うのか。細部の検討の結果がこのポケモンが「いる感じ」を作り出す。
[右]《コイキング》の着彩 | 素焼したボディに顔料を加えた釉薬を施し、その後本焼へ。作者の求める「らしさ」が徐々に可視化されていく。

[left] Forming *Venusaur* | Just clay, with such power! For example, what about the eyelids over the spherical eyes? How far can we follow the mouth, the depths of the ears? Imai's careful consideration of the details produced this Pokémon with its sense of presence.
[right] Applying color to *Magikarp* | Glaze to which pigments have been added is applied over the bisque-fired body, and then it is fired again (glost firing). The “essence” that the artist seeks is gradually becoming visible.

フシギバナ Venusaur　ゼニガメ Squirtle　アーボック Arbok　キングラー Kingler　コイキング Magikarp

似合うとにらんで、“縄”にも力を入れました。自然と人工、現実とフィクションの協働が「らしさ」を高めています。

•

陶器：焼物の一種。非透光性で若干の吸水性がある。土物とも。磁器と比べ厚手で重さがあり、叩いたときの音も鈍い。焼成温度は土器より高く、磁器より低い1100～1300℃程度。一般に粘土や長石などの原料を配合し、低火度で焼き締めた（素焼）のち施釉(せゆう)し、より高い温度で焼成（本焼）する。

•

"Essence"

Imai Sadamasa was born in the third generation of a family of potters. After a childhood in which he was handed clay and played with it in a corner of the studio, he decided, at an early age, to make ceramics himself. That was because, with living beings as his motifs, he discovered traits that ceramics had in common with them, in the feel of the clay and the luster of the glazes. It is also true that, among living beings, what he particularly likes are cold-blooded animals. Frogs, snakes, lizards, turtles, green iguanas, all of which he raised. His life today is still shared with "some creature."

As a result of studying the elements making up both those animals and ceramics, he creates in a style often described as realistic. Imai says, however, "That is not my key word. I express the "essence" of the motif." That is his main point. "Measuring the subject, taking a mold of it, and creating a work, and it will be utterly without life. To state it drastically, making something in an entirely different shape and having people say it looks just like whatever is my ideal." Imai builds the essence extracted from his motif. That makes someone else recall fragments of memory, connect them, and are made to experience what his work is about. An interplay of images occurs through the work, bringing surprise and enjoyment of discovery.

•

Making a Plus

Imai's working style begins with hand building, then trimming and correcting the body, adding more clay, and finishing the work. He makes it clear that he is thinking about his object in the "plus work of adding clay."

This time, Imai seemed to enjoy making the details of the *Venusaur*'s mouth quite a bit. While looking at every corner of his work, we are overwhelmed by the shading drifting with the unevenness of the skin. If we met this **Venusaur**, having been led there by aroma wafting from its flower... Facing its dignified appearance, one's heart rings with a story that is one's own.

Imai also thinks of applying the glaze as part of the modeling process. For **Arbok**, Imai used only the *tamagusuri* (Kutani ware's glaze), and fired the overglaze enamels five times. "If you apply the same overglaze enamel all over and fire it once, it often looks kind of like a simple toy. But if you apply glaze over it, touch it up, and fire it again and again, gradually a depth develops."

Kingler is riding a kind of float. "The artificial object and the natural object work together extremely well. The combination is one you might find washed upon the beach." Kingler, a water-type Pokémon with claws, resembles a crab. For that connection Imai also stressed the rope. The collaboration between natural and artificial, fact and fiction, enhances the work's "essence."

•

Ceramics: A type of pottery. Opaque and somewhat porous, it is thicker and heavier than porcelain and sounds dull when struck. The firing temperature is higher than earthenware and lower than porcelain, at 1,100–1,300°C. Usually made with a mixture of materials, including clay and feldspar. After the body is fired at a low temperature (bisque firing) and then glazed, it is fired again at a higher temperature (glost firing).

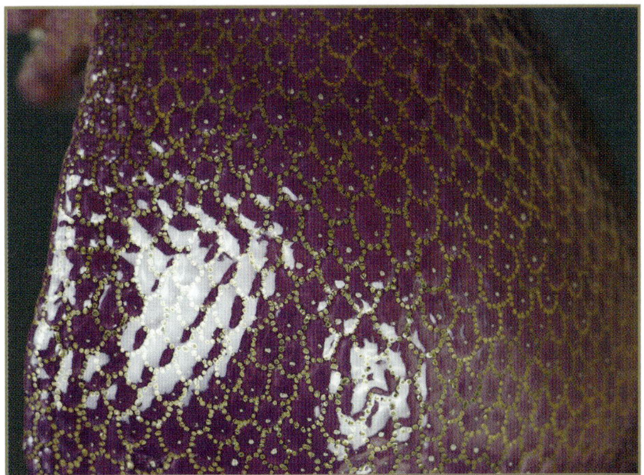

[上]《アーボック》（背面部分）｜コブラポケモンらしくアーボックには鱗のような表層を想定。敵を怯えさせるというお腹の模様だけでなく、背面までぬかりなし。全身に金彩で無数の小さな点も打った。「アーボックの“鱗”は特にがんばったところ」。
[下]《ゼニガメ》の甲羅も負けていない。「とじこもり みを まもる」だけでなく、釉薬と金彩でうっとりする輝きに。

[top] *Arbok* (back) | The assumption was that Arbok, the Cobra Pokémon, would have scales. Not just the pattern on its belly, which would frighten enemies, but the back, too, is flawless. To create the scales, Imai applied countless small dots of gold pigment over the entire creature. "I worked particularly hard on *Arbok*'s scales."
[bottom] Not only does *Squirtle*'s shell offer it protection, but Imai used glaze and gold pigment to give it a charming gleam.

葉山有樹　Hayama Yuki

森羅万象ポケモン壷｜Vase with Pokémon of the Universe

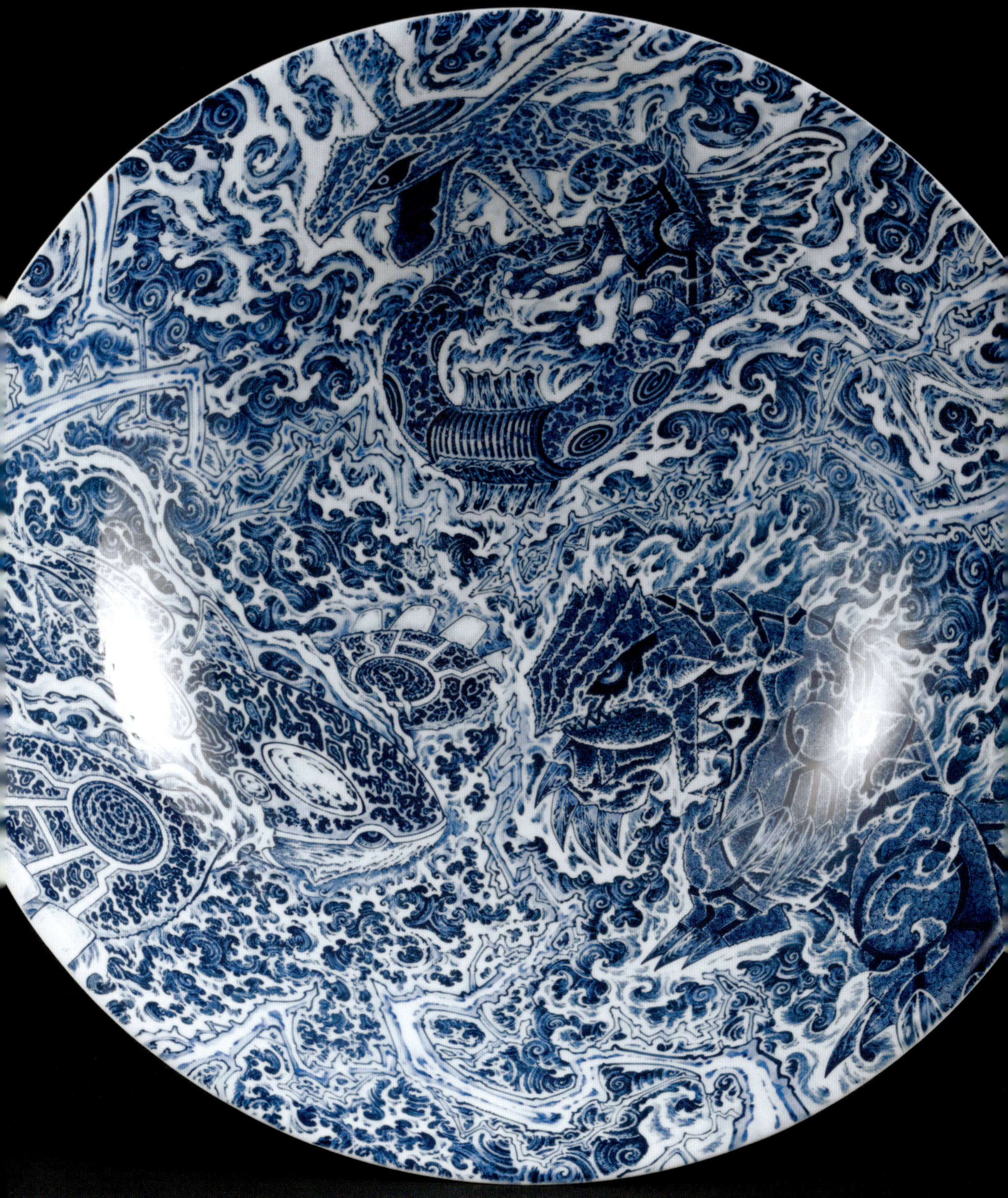

超古代ポケモン玉盌｜
Beautiful Bowl with the Super-Ancient of Pokémon

陶磁
Ceramics

葉山有樹
Hayama Yuki

●

描く／書く

葉山有樹は日本を代表する窯業地の１つ、佐賀県有田で生まれ、15歳で焼きものの製造会社に就職しました。轆轤の工程から修業を始め、入社3年目に絵付をする部署に異動。量産を求められる現場で1日に同じ文様を1200個分描き続けたこともあるそうです。その厳しさは疲労骨折を引き起こしたくらい…。が、23歳で起業する前に通った経験が「仕事をするための身体」を作り、今日“超絶技巧”とも呼ばれる技の礎となったのだと葉山は振り返ります。

それと同時に葉山は、伝統の名のもとに形骸化した文様、そして焼きものの歴史を掘り起こすことを求めました。それは源流を辿り、瑞々しさを取り戻した制作対象を自身の座標軸に置きなおす作業。「著述家」というもう１つの肩書は、陶芸の道に向かう葉山の姿勢を明らかにするようです。

●

出現

《超古代ポケモン玉盌》がモチーフとしたのは、九州に似たホウエン地方に伝わる物語。天、地、海を司る**レックウザ**、**グラードン**、**カイオーガ**が揃った緊迫の瞬間に、固唾をのまずにいられません。実はこの作品は、呉須の青の深さを追求して1320℃の焼成を2回行ったところ、残念ながら1度は大破してしまったのですが、それでも強烈な気迫が欠片からも立ち昇るほどだったのが印象的でした。みごとに完成した今、鉢に内包される轆轤の回転運動が底から口縁まで広がって、太古のエネルギーをことさらに拡張させます。

《森羅万象ポケモン壷》に目を移すと、こちらは満ち満ちる豊かさを掌で受け止めたくなる球体です。更紗で知られる「アラス・アラサン文様」は、森で育まれた動植物を図様化したもの。その根源的な願いに心を寄せた葉山の「森羅万象図」シリーズがポケモン×工芸に登場しました。壷の表面を余すところなく描き込まれたのは無数の植物、そして500匹を超えるポケモンたち。確実に種類を描き分けながらも完全に調和する様子は、生命の源の秘密を知らせるかのようでもあります。染付でモチーフの表情を生き生きと写し取り、藍の陰影が潤んで視線を内へと誘う一方、本焼に際してかけた透明釉、泥漿（陶土に水を混ぜ、液状やクリーム状にしたもの）と釉を混ぜ、剣先と筆で盛り上げた白線や点描、そして金彩は、繰り返し焼成する都度さまざまな光の質を作品に与えました。壷の表層というわずかな厚みに築かれた奥行感が鑑賞する心理に働きかけ、顔を寄せ、また耳をそばだてたくなる思いがします。

アトリエにて。激しくぶつかり合うポケモン3匹の古代の気が鉢の外側まで迸［ほとばし］る。
In the studio. The ancient powers of the three Pokémon, which clash violently, spill out to the exterior of the bowl.

●

ホウエン地方に伝わる神話：遥か昔、ホウエンに強大な力を有した2匹のポケモンが現れた。グラードンが吠えると大地が盛り上がり、陸が広がった。太陽が照りつけて、灼熱が辺りを包んだ。カイオーガの咆哮で水が溢れ出し、海が広がった。暗雲が立ち込め、豪雨となった。両者は度々衝突を繰り返し、ホウエンの人々やポケモンの暮らしを脅かしたが、そこに神と崇められていた天空に住まうポケモンのレックウザが現れ、争いを鎮めたといわれている。

●

An Artist and a Storyteller

Hayama Yuki was born in Arita, Saga, one of Japan's leading ceramics production areas, and began working for a pottery manufacturing company at the age of 15. He began his training on a potter's wheel, and in his third year with the company he was transferred to the painting department. On a job requiring mass production, he once painted the same pattern on 1,200 pieces in a single day. The rigors of the job were so severe that he suffered

アンノーン
Unown

カイオーガ
Kyogre

グラードン
Groudon

レックウザ
Rayquaza

a bone fracture from fatigue. However, Hayama recalls that the experience he went through before starting his own business at the age of 23 helped him build a "body made for work," and this underpins the exquisite artistry that characterized his work today.

Meanwhile, Hayama has sought to uncover the history of patterns that have stagnated due to tradition, and the history of pottery itself. This is a process of retracing the origins of pottery and placing the objects , which have regained their freshness and vigor, on his own axes of coordinates. In addition to "artist," his other title, "storyteller," seems to reveal Hayama's stance toward his own path of ceramic art.

•

Arrival

Beautiful Bowl with the Super-Ancient Pokémon is inspired by a legend from Hoenn, a region of the Pokémon world that is similar to Kyushu, a southern region of Japan. One cannot help holding one's breath at the tense moment when **Rayquaza**, **Groudon**, and **Kyogre**, the legendary Pokémon representing sky, land, and sea respectively, appear all at once. In fact, this piece was fired twice at 1320 °C so as to maximize the depth of the cobalt-based blue *gosu* pigment, and unfortunately one of these times it shattered, but it was still so impressive that an intense spirit rose even from the shards. Now that it has been successfully completed, the rotational movement of the potter's wheel inherent in the bowl extends from the bottom to the rim, expanding the energy of prehistoric times even further.

Turning to *Vase with Pokémon of the Universe*, we see a spherical vessel that makes you want to take its abundant fullness in your hands. The *alas alasan* pattern, also known from calico, comprises plants and animals nurtured by the forest. Hayama's Universe series is inspired by this primal drive, and now it appears in *Pokémon x Kogei*. The surface of the vase is covered with countless plants and over 500 Pokémon. The way in which the different species are rendered in perfect harmony, while scrupulously kept separate, seems to let us in on a secret about the original source of life. While the subjects' expressions are vividly rendered in underglaze blue, shades of indigo beckon the viewer's gaze inward, and transparent glaze, slurry (ceramic clay mixed with water to form a creamy liquid,) and glaze mixed with a sharp utensil and brush are used to create white lines, dots, and gold paint which were applied at the time of the second firing, giving a range of luminous qualities to the repeatedly fired work. The sense of depth embedded in the slight thickness of the vase's surface works on the viewer's psyche, making him or her want to draw closer to the vase and listen closely.

•

Legend of the Hoenn Region: Long, long ago, two Pokémon of great power appeared in the Hoenn region. Groudon howled, the ground rose, and the land expanded. The sun shone and a scorching heat enveloped the area; Kyogre's roar caused the waters to overflow and the sea to spread. Dark clouds rolled in and torrential rains fell. The two clashed often, threatening the lives of the people and Pokémon of the Hoenn region, until Rayquaza, the revered sky-dwelling Pokémon, appeared and quelled the conflict.

1

2

3

❶図案｜モチーフ個々の形姿を検証したのち、平面から球体への展開を考える。
❷染付書き（青花）｜900°Cで素焼したボディに呉須（酸化コバルトを主成分とする顔料）で文様を描く。ざらついた吸水性も高い面に緻密な文様を描くには恐ろしく高度な技術を要する。下書きはなくフリーハンド。極細の線もしばしばほかと同じ筆で、穂先の先端に全神経を注ぎながら描く。濃［だ］みは面に呉須の溶液を染み込ませる技法で、にじみを防ぐのは先に書いた線のかすかな隆起のみ。立ち上がった口にアンノーンを発見!
❸高台の中にもパラダイスが続く。

❶ Design drawing | After examining the shapes of individual motifs, Hayama explored its development from a flat surface to a sphere.
❷ *Sometsuke* firing (*seika*) | After examining the shapes of individual motifs, the artist explored their development from flat to spherical and painted patterns on the body, which was fired unglazed at 900°C, using *gosu* pigment mainly composed of cobalt oxide. Painting a precise pattern on a rough, highly absorbent surface requires an extremely high level of skill. He paints freehand with no underpainting. Often he makes even ultra-fine lines with the same brush as the others, with all his attention focused on the tip of the utensil. The technique of *dami* involves staining the surface with a solution of *gosu*, and only the faint ridges of the previously painted lines prevent the color from bleeding. Unown appears on the elongated mouth of the vase!
❸ Paradise is depicted on the bottom of the base.

Stories — Jump in!

2 ものがたり — 浸る！

ポケモンの世界観に工芸が挑戦しました。捕獲や育成、進化、交換などの要素がもたらすワクワク感。冒険の舞台への憧れや、旅の仲間たちと育んだ友情。あるいは固唾をのんで見守った技のインパクト。仮想世界であってもそこで得た感興はリアルで、そして現実世界と通底する根源的な何かもありそう…。作家たちは工芸の素材と技とを携えて、想像のフィールドを駆けめぐりました。作品を介し、ポケモンと工芸のふたつの物語を行き来する喜びがここにあります。

The craft challenged the world of Pokémon. The excitement brought about by components such as catching, training, evolving, and trading Pokémon. The longing for the stage of adventure and the friendships nurtured with fellow travelers. Or the impact of the moves we watched with bated breath. Even though it is a virtual world, the excitement felt there is real, and there may be something fundamental to the real world as well. The artists traveled the imaginary field with their craft materials and techniques. Through their works, you will have the pleasure of traveling back and forth between the two stories of Pokémon and craft.

田中信行 Tanaka Nobuyuki

無題 | Untitled

田中信行

Tanaka Nobuyuki

•

ゾクッ

ポケモンの技の１つに「かげうち」があります。ゴーストタイプに具わり、自身の影を伸ばして相手の背後に回り込んで攻撃します。「ふいうち」や「であいがしら」同様に先制攻撃技、そして物理技に分類されますが、かげうちではその言外にも思いをめぐらせたくなるのはどうしたことでしょう。効果を発揮するのがエスパータイプやゴーストタイプのポケモンに対してというのも興味深いし、そもそも黒々としたものが知らぬ間に足元を潜り抜け、後ろで高く伸び上がる事態がわが身にふりかかったとしたら…。ポケモンがそうであるように、その技もまた、自然から人工のさまざまな事物に目を向ける契機をもたらします。かげうちでいえば、やはり「影」という要素が私たちの想像を掻き立てるようです。

•

漆黒

日本語でこれ以上ない深い黒を意味する語。「漆黒の闇」ともいうように、光を吸収する黒に漆という物質名が付くだけで、闇の粒子が肌に触れるような奇妙な感覚が沸き起り、安穏とした日常から私たちを切り離します。

今回、田中信行は、この漆黒の概念を通して、ポケモンの技「かげうち」を考えることに挑戦しました。かげうちの得体の知れなさは、まさに漆黒の闇にも通ずる根源的な恐怖と重なるようにも見えます。しかし、そもそも影には実体はなく、一方、工芸は実材研究の結晶ともいえる造形です。そのあいだを橋渡ししたのは漆を見ることによる心理作用であり、それは田中が長年追い続けている漆の虚実にほかなりません。

2メートルを超える大作と対峙した人は、視界に映る現象の捉えがたさにクラクラするかもしれません。この物質感特有の透明感が、黒の奥へと視線を誘って距離感を見失わせるのです。光沢が表層を走り、輪郭を断定するのも難しいほど。題名はあえての《無題》。名前をもたない不確実性が、想像の余地を無限にしました。

「かげうち」のエフェクトイメージ
“Shadow Sneak” effect image

•

乾漆

漆工における成形法の一種。漆を塗りながら型に麻布を貼り重ね、必要な厚みを得てから型から外します。軽く堅牢さに優れ、近代では塑造特有の柔らかみをもった自由な形が探求されるようになりました。

田中が本作で狙ったのは「地面からつき上がる『かげ』の流れるような造形」です。影には絶対値はありません。だからこの世に存在する具体的な何ものにも頼らないかたち。それでいてどこか心の奥底で繋がっているような感覚をもたらしもします。見る角度で光と陰影とがよどみなく移り変わり、認知の可能性を問いただします。

•

漆：ウルシ科ウルシの樹液。樹皮に傷をつけ、にじみ出てきたところを採取する。不透明な乳白色で、空気に触れると茶褐色になる。主成分はウルシオール。アジアで広く使われ、日本では縄文時代の遺跡からも漆器が見つかっている。一般に「漆が乾く」といい、「乾漆」の技法名にも「乾」の文字が用いられるが、乾燥したなかでは漆は固まらない。「漆が乾く」ことの実際は、空気中の水分から取り込んだ酸素とウルシオールが化学反応を起こして、液体から固体になった状態。そのため漆の硬化には75〜80％という高湿度、また温度も20〜30℃の環境を要する。

•

Thrills and Chills

One of the battle moves, common to Ghost-type Pokémon, is Shadow Sneak, in which a Pokémon extends its shadow to attack an opponent from behind. Like Sucker Punch and First Impression, it is a preemptive, physical move, but what is it about the

Shadow Sneak that conveys something beyond its words? It is interesting to note that it works against Psychic-type and Ghost-type Pokémon, and it would be even more interesting to see what would happen to us if something dark were to sneak under our feet and tower up behind us without our knowing it... Like Pokémon themselves, their moves also direct our attention to diverse phenomena, from the natural to the manmade. With Shadow Sneak, the element of "shadow" seems to capture our imaginations.

•

Shikkoku

In Japanese the word *shikkoku*, literally "*urushi* lacquer black," means black that could not be any darker. The mere combination of the characters for "*urushi*" and "black," which absorbs light, evokes a strange sensation as if particles of darkness are clinging to our skin, separating us from our peaceful daily lives.

Here, Tanaka Nobuyuki challenges us to see the Pokémon move Shadow Sneak in terms of this conception of jet-blackness. The mysterious nature of Shadow Sneak seems to overlap with an atavistic fear of total darkness. However, shadows fundamentally have no substance, while craft is an art form that grows out of research into physical materials. What bridges the gap between the two is the psychological effect of viewing *urushi*, and this is the fact and fiction of *urushi* that Tanaka has been pursuing for many years.

Viewers of this monumental work over two meters high may feel dizzy at the elusiveness of the phenomenon in their field of vision. The transparency peculiar to *urushi*'s materiality beckons the viewer's gaze deep into the blackness, making it impossible to gauge distance. The glossy coating of the surface layer makes it difficult even to determine the outline of the work. The work is deliberately untitled, and the uncertainty of having no name leaves infinite room for imagination.

•

Kanshitsu (Dried *Urushi* Lacquer)

A molding technique used in *urushi* lacquer work. Linen is layered over the mold while applying *urushi*, and once the required thickness has been achieved, the mold is removed. It is light yet sturdy, and in modern times artists have freely explored forms with the flexibility characteristic of the molding process.

Tanaka's goal with this work was to create "the flowing form of a shadow rising from the ground." Shadows have no absolute qualities. They are shapes with no reliance on any existing physical form, and yet they give us a sense of connection somewhere deep inside. Light and shadows shift without hesitation depending on the angle of view, causing us to question the possibilities of cognition.

•

❶マケット｜1/4と1/2.4スケールで2回作成。材料は原型と同じく発泡スチロール。面のしなやかさやエッジの効きとともに陰影の現れ方も検証する。
❷原型｜発泡スチロールを削り出す。表面を丁寧に整えてから次の作業へと進む。
❸布貼り・下地｜麻布を漆で塗り重ねて成形。田中の脳裏でイメージの陰影が一層濃くなっていく。
❹上塗り｜漆を重ねるたびに被膜の美しさが更新される。[動画『田中信行／Nobuyuki Tanaka』2018年, directed by Masato Mitsunari (totem) より]

❶ Maquettes | Two maquettes are made, at 1/4 and 1/2.4 scale. Like the prototype, they are made of styrene foam. They enable verification of how the shading looks, as well as the suppleness of the surface and the crispness of the edges.
❷ Prototype | Made by carving styrene foam. The surface is carefully prepared before proceeding to the next step.
❸ Fabric application and base coats | The image is formed by applying *urushi* to layers of linen, and the image grows even darker in Tanaka's mind.
❹ Top coats | The beauty of the coating deepens with each layer of *urushi*. [From the video *Nobuyuki Tanaka*, 2018, directed by Masato Mitsunari (totem)].

Urushi lacquer: The sap of the *urushi* lacquer tree, obtained by cutting into the bark and collecting the sap as it oozes out. It is an opaque milky white, and turns brown when exposed to air. The active ingredient is known as urushiol. *Urushi* is widely used across Asia, and *urushi* lacquerware has been found at prehistoric Jomon Period (ca. 14,500 to 13,000-400 BCE) sites in Japan. People speak of *urushi* drying, and the character for "dry" also appears in the name of the *kanshitsu* technique, but *urushi* does not actually harden in dry conditions. Actually, it turns from a liquid to a solid when urushiol reacts chemically with oxygen from moisture in the air. Thus *urushi* requires high humidity of 75-80% and a temperature of 20-30°C to harden.

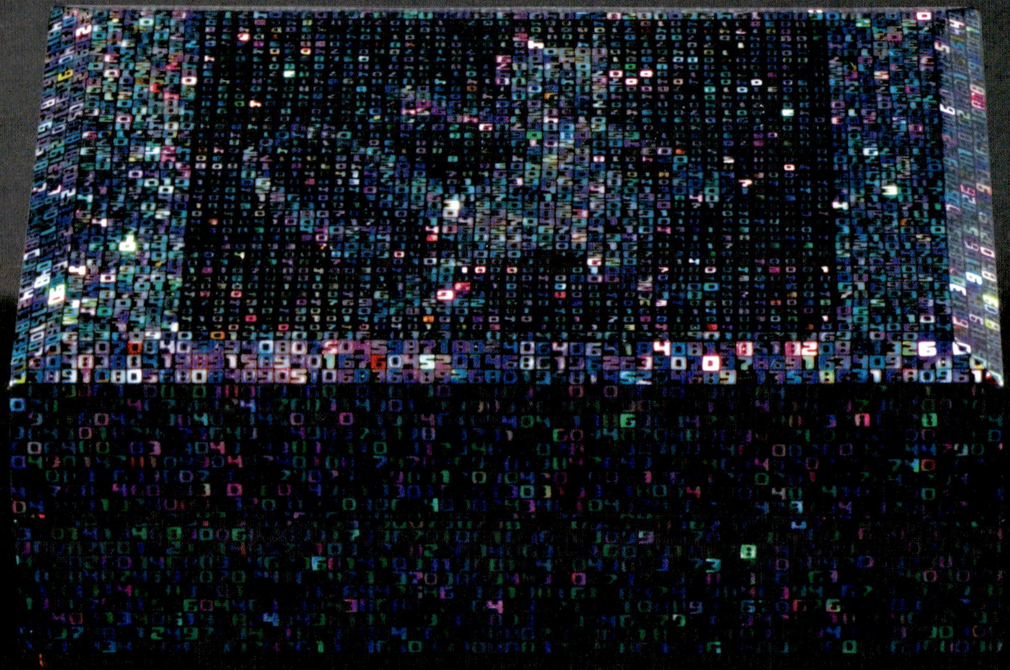

池田晃将　Ikeda Terumasa

百千光絵素飾箱「壱伍零」|
Ornamental Box, "Mewtwo", Luminous Design, *Raden* Inlay

未知文黒御影茶器 |
Tea Caddy, Unown Design, Black Granite Style

電線光環中次 | Tea Caddy, Electric Exchange Design

漆工
Lacquerware

池田晃将
Ikeda Terumasa

螺鈿

もともと池田晃将が関心を抱いていたのは装飾美術や宗教建築でした。「金沢に住んでみたい」と考え、金沢美術工芸大学で漆芸を専攻、現在も市内で工房を開いています。とはいえ古来の技法をスタイルもそのままに継承したのでは意味がない。そこでテーマとしたのが「情報」。「(具体的な姿かたちは)目に見えないが、現代では人の心の拠りどころとなる」と考えたからでした。そして「目に見えない」ことの表現手段として選んだのが螺鈿です。螺鈿は夜光貝、アワビ貝、蝶貝などの真珠層を研ぎ出して板状に加工し、漆で接着する装飾法。「螺」は貝を、「鈿」はちりばめるを意味します。

伝統的には動植物をかたどったパーツを貼って装飾した例が多いのですが、池田作品では極小の幾何学形態や数字などが器物全面を覆います。脳内を一瞬のうちに走る信号を直感させるこの描法で、今回池田が挑戦したモチーフは**ヒトカゲ・ゼニガメ・フシギダネ**、さらに**ミュウツー**、**アンノーン**、そしてモンスターボール。『ポケットモンスター 赤・緑』で最初のパートナーポケモンを選んだり、「交換」システムに接したときのワクワク感。遺伝子工学を駆使して生みだされたというミュウツーのドラマ。眺めるうちに意味を読み取れそうなアンノーンの神秘。どんなサイズのポケモンも捕らえるモンスターボールの驚異。螺鈿が放つ光の刺激が私たちの記憶を呼び覚まし、目と心を釘付けにします。

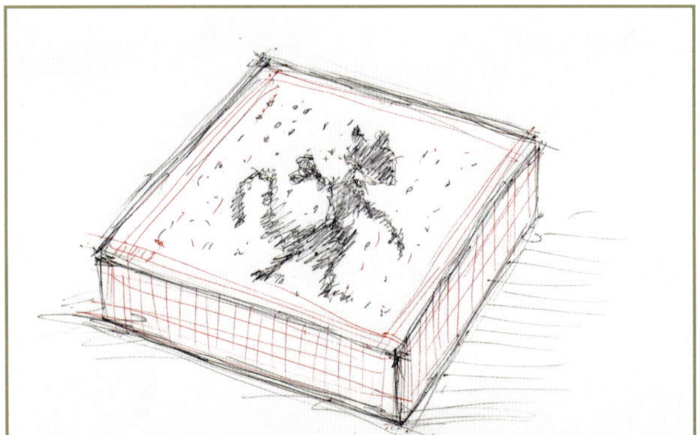

ラフデザイン|《百千光絵素飾箱「壱伍零」》
Rough design: *Ornamental Box, "Mewtwo," Luminous Design, Raden Inlay*

箱

物の保管や輸送に用いる容器。小学校で習う「箱」以外にも函、匣、筥、筐など多様な漢字が使い分けられます。日本では箱は調度の要。善美を尽くして拵えたものは、内容物が失われたあとも大切に取りおかれ、伝世品のなかには国宝や重要文化財の指定を受けるものもあります。

箱がそれほどまでに美しく装わされるのは、本来的には"中"を想う心の表れにほかなりません。たとえ「飾箱」と命名したとしても、直方体の塊ではなく、蓋と身による構造体とするのは、きっと内包する空間に象徴的な価値を見いだすから。そうした事がらを鑑みても、「モンスターボール」は箱制作の主題にぴったりでした。物語のさまざまな局面を展開させるモンスターボール、そして箱というオブジェクト。どちらも興味が尽きない存在です。

Raden

Ikeda Terumasa was originally interested in decorative arts and religious architecture. He decided that he "wanted to live in Kanazawa," majored in *urushi* lacquer art at the Kanazawa College of Art, and still maintains a studio in the city. However, he felt it would be meaningless to carry on an ancient technique with no stylistic changes. With this in mind, he settled on the theme of "information." This was because he thought of it as "invisible (in concrete form), but in the current era it is a source of nourishment for people's hearts and minds." To express this "invisible" thing he chose *raden*, a decorative technique in which the nacreous layers of turban shells, abalone, and pearl oysters are ground into a plate-like form and affixed to *urushi*. The "*ra*" in *raden* means "seashell," and "*den*" means "inlaid."

Traditionally, pieces are often decorated with bits of pearly shell to form the shapes of plants and animals, but in Ikeda's work, minuscule geometric shapes and numerals cover the entire surfaces of containers. Using this technique, which evokes signals instantaneously running through the brain, he depicted **Charmander**, **Squirtle**, **Bulbasaur**, **Mewtwo**, **Unown**, and a Poké Ball. There is a sense of excitement akin to that of selecting one's first partner Pokémon in the *Pokémon Red and Pokémon Blue*, or of engaging with the "trading" system. The drama of Mewtwo, created through genetic engineering. The mystery of Unown, which seems to take on layers of meaning as you gaze at it. The wonders of the Poké

フシギダネ
Bulbasaur

ヒトカゲ
Charmander

ゼニガメ
Squirtle

ミュウツー
Mewtwo

アンノーン
Unown

❶3D CADで設計した形を特注のレーザーカッターで薄貝にミシン目のような微細な穴を開ける。このあと超音波洗浄機に入れ、水中に伝わる微震でパーツを抜き出す。
❷全面漆塗りした箱に貝のパーツを貼っていく。数字パーツのサイズや漆地の黒の分量の差異が明暗と光沢の質をコントロールし、蓋にミュウツーの姿が現れた。
❸研ぎ出し。御影石風のテクスチャーのなかでアンノーンの姿が顕わになる。奥から浮かび上がるような効果が、発掘品を思わせる独特の雰囲気を濃くする。
❹蓋の中面と身の立ち上がり部分には蒔絵を、内底にも螺鈿を施す(《百千光絵素飾箱「壱伍零」》)。蓋を開けると新たな驚きと喜びが広がる美しい仕掛け。
❺思わず手に取りたくなるサイズ感。垂直面と水平面が掌の上で角度を変えながら、構造色の魅力を振りまいている。

❶ A custom-made laser cutter is used to make microscopic perforations designed with 3D CAD in a thin layer of shell. After this, the shell is placed in an ultrasonic washer, and the parts are extracted by micro-vibrations transmitted into the water.
❷ Shell parts are affixed to a box that has been completely coated with *urushi*. Differences in the sizes of the numeral parts and the amount of black in the *urushi* ground modulate the qualities of light and dark and luster, and the figure of Mewtwo appears on the lid.
❸ Sanding to a smooth finish. The figure of Unown is revealed in the granite-like texture. The effect of stone emerging from the depths deepens the unique atmosphere of the piece, which is reminiscent of an excavated artifact.
❹ The inside of the lid and the edges of the body of *Ornamental Box, "Mewtwo," Luminous Design, Raden Inlay* are decorated with *maki-e* (gold or silver dust sprinkled on *urushi*), and the bottom of the interior with *raden* inlay. This beautiful mechanism delivers surprise and delight when the lid is opened.
❺ This piece fits right in the palm, making one instinctively want to pick it up. When the angles of vertical and horizontal surfaces change in the hand, the structural colors emanate delightful effects.

Ball to catch Pokémons of any size. The luminous stimulus of *raden* awakens memories, captivating the viewer's eyes and heart.

•

Boxes

Boxes are containers used for storing and transporting things. In Japan the word "box" is written with various *kanji*, not only the standard 箱 learned in elementary school, but also others with varying nuances such as 函, 匣, 筥, and 筐. In Japan, the box is the basic unit of furnishings. Boxes made with the utmost care and beauty are treasured even after the contents are gone, and some historic items have been designated National Treasures or Important Cultural Properties.

The fact that boxes are so beautifully decorated essentially reflects a mentality of treasuring what is "inside" them. Even if a box is called a "decorative box," it is not a solid rectilinear mass but a structure with a body and a lid, because of the symbolic value ascribed to the space it contains. In light of these observations, the Poké Ball was the perfect subject for creation of a box. There is endless intrigue to both the Poké Ball, which unfolds multifaceted aspects of the story, and the box as an object.

新實広記　Niimi Hiroki

Vessel -TSURARA- | Vessel -TSURARA-

新實広記
Niimi Hiroki

空間・VESSEL

新實広記の仕事の多くはインスタレーションとして発表されます。インスタレーションの原義は「設置」。作品を取り巻く環境への関心を進め、展示する空間全体を作品とみなす手法です。大学進学前から建築に興味があったという新實の制作は、アクションを仕掛ける“場”を訪ねることから始まります。そこで最適解とするボリュームを検討。ふだんは物語性を想定しない新實ですが、今回はポケモンの技である「つららおとし」が挑戦のテーマ。

そこで新實が選んだキーワードは「2つのリアリティ」です。一方はガラスという物質がもたらす果てしない魅力。他方はポケモンの技の現場に立ち会うスリル。展示空間に入り、作品を覗き込むことで、2つの体験の往来を企図しました。さらに新實は、そこにきわめて日本的な「見立て」のセンスが介入することを予測。感覚を呼び込む“器”の精度を高めるべく、ガラスに内包される光を確かめながら表面の磨き作業は繰り返し行われました。

つららおとし

文字通り氷柱状の塊が天空から落下して、対戦相手にダメージをもたらします。想像するだけで恐ろしいようですが、新實は氷柱が落下する直前に、天空に光の花々が開くエフェクトにも注目しました。《Vessel –TSURARA–》はまさにこの現象が結晶化した空間となりました。とてつもない重量、尖った形状、エッジの硬さ、なのにワレモノ注意の繊細さ。それでいて内にたたえた光の相は見飽きず、表面はマットもクリアも皮膚をざわめかせる。微細な泡は液体だった物質の記憶をほのめかす。恐怖と美しさがないまぜになったスリルを体感し、ふたたびかの技のエフェクトを思い出します。

つららおとし｜こおりタイプの技で、くさタイプ、じめんタイプ、ひこうタイプ、ドラゴンタイプのポケモンに対して優位。「大きな氷柱を激しくぶつけて攻撃する。相手をひるませることがある」。
Icicle Crash | This is an Ice-type move, which gives it an advantage over Grass-type, Ground-type, Flying-type, and Dragon-type Pokémon. The user attacks by crashing large icicles onto the target. This may also make the target flinch.

Space / Vessel

Much of Niimi Hiroki's work is presented in the form of installations, a word that is of course originally derived from the verb "to install." With this approach, artists take their interests in the environment surrounding their works one step further and regard the entire space where it is exhibited as part of the work. Having been interested in architecture since before university, Niimi's process begins with a visit to the "place" where the action will occur. He then considers volumes that will achieve an optimal solution. Niimi does not normally plan out a narrative, but this time he took on the theme of Icicle Crash, a Pokémon move.

The keywords he chose were "two realities": the endless fascination of glass as a material, and the thrill of being present at the site of a Pokémon move. By entering the gallery and peering into the works, visitors may be able to traverse these two experiences. Niimi anticipates that a very Japanese sense of "substitution" will intervene. To enhance the precision of the "vessels" that beckons the senses, he repeatedly polished their surfaces while checking the quality of light contained in the glass.

Icicle Crash

With this move, icicle-shaped chunks fall from the sky, causing damage to opponents. As frightening as it sounds, Niimi also focused on the effects of light spreading across the sky just before icicles fall. His *Vessel –TSURARA–* [Icicle] is a space in which this very phenomenon is crystallized. The unimaginable weight, the pointed shape, the hard edges, and yet the delicacy of the piece. But still it never makes us tired of looking at the light that is inside. The surfaces, both matte and transparent, seem to act directly on the observer's skin. Tiny bubbles hint at the memory of a substance that used to be liquid. The viewer experiences a thrill of combined fear and beauty, and is once again reminded of the effects of the Icicle Crash.

❶構想｜個々の形とサイズ、組み合わせのバランス、それらを総合的に「ボリューム」として理解し、空間と心理に与える作用を同時に検討。発泡スチロールや光を含む透明な素材を切り出して試してみる。
❷原型｜発泡スチロールの塊を切り出し、ペーパーで磨いて形を決める。この原型をもとに耐火石膏で鋳型[いがた]を作成する。
❸窯入れ準備｜ビレット(ガラス塊)を鋳型内に詰め、さらに湯口と呼ばれる注ぎ口を耐火石膏で設けてここにも詰める。半球形のビレットがかさばって鋳型内に十分な量が収まらないので、湯口からも熔けたガラスが流れ込む仕組み。耐火石膏製の鋳型の周りは熱衝撃に強いセメントで補強してある。100kgを超えるガラスが熔けると、鋳型に大きな圧力がかかるため。
❹割り出し｜慎重に型を割って取り出す。一番好きな瞬間。「型が崩れずにガラスが流れているかを確認する。発泡スチロールで見ていた形がガラスに生まれ変わる瞬間」。
❺磨き｜研磨機を使って形を整える。最初は粗い80番のダイヤモンドパッドで「ガラス表皮を削り取るイメージ」。その後、徐々に目の細かいものに変えて艶を出していく。最後は砂目の粗いものに戻して手磨き。全体のマットな質感を整える。満足のいくまで繰り返し磨き続ける。

❶ Conception | The shapes and sizes of individual parts and the balance of their combination are comprehensively understood as "volumes," and their spatial and psychological effects are examined. Niimi cuts and experiments with styrene foam and transparent, luminous materials.
❷ Prototype | A block of styrene foam is cut and sanded to shape it. Based on this prototype, a mold is made from fire-resistant plaster.
❸ Preparation for firing | A mold is filled with billets (chunks of glass), and a spout made of fire-resistant plaster is prepared and also filled. As the hemispherical billets are too bulky to fill the mold with a sufficient volume of glass, molten glass is poured in through the spout as well. The fire-resistant plaster mold is reinforced with thermal shock-resistant cement to withstand the great pressure exerted on the molds when more than 100 kg of glass is melted.
❹ Removal from mold | The mold is carefully broken and the cast object removed. This is his favorite moment: "Checking to see if the glass has flowed without losing its shape. The moment when the form I saw in the styrene foam is transformed into glass."
❺ Polishing | Refining the shape with a power sander. At first, a coarse 80-grit diamond sanding pad is used "as if scraping off the surface skin of the glass." Then he gradually shifts to finer grit to make it shiny. Finally, he goes back to coarser-grit sandpaper for polishing by hand. The overall matte texture is then refined. This polishing process is repeated until he is satisfied with the results.

池本一三　Ikemoto Kazumi

湖のほとりで | By the Lake

ガラス
Glass Works

池本一三
Ikemoto Kazumi

旅する

これまでほとんど携帯型ゲーム機を触わったことがなかった池本一三。今回手にした『ポケットモンスター ソード・シールド』で、初めてゲームというものを体験したそうです。作品制作のためにリクエストをすれば、シーンでもポケモンの細部でも資料提供を受けることができました。情報の確認であれば、その手続きで事足りたのかもしれません。「でもそれだけではダメ」。そういえば以前ガラス制作に関するテキストで、池本はこんなことを書いていました。「対象物に対して自分がどのように感じているかを知ることが、ドローイングをする上で重要なことなのです」。ついに殿堂入りまで果たしたという長い長いゲームプレイは、おそらくは筆記具の代わりにゲーム機を用いた、見て、感じて、考える時間。フィクションゆえに求めた「体験」は、そのままポケモンとアーティスト・池本一三、それぞれの世界観を融合させるプロセスとなりました。

作品の舞台はガラル地方。ポケモントレーナーの少年と仲間たち＝池本がプレイ中に選んだポケモンたちの、ハロンタウンからシュートシティにいたる冒険が綴られました。3章だての立体絵巻には、ポケモンファンにとって馴染み深いランドマークと、池本らしい風景描写とがシームレスに展開し、まだ見ぬ先へと誘うようです。

光・光・光

旅の思い出を歌い上げる豊かな色調。使ったのは赤、黄、緑は3色、青が2色、ペールオレンジの計8色。8色だけで？ と思わず聞き返したくなるほどの多彩さは、エナメル描法で実現しました。エナメルは金属化合物を低温でガラスに焼き付けられるように調合した材料で、池本はアルコールに溶かし、ガラス面に吹き付けて使います。1色ずつ吹き付け、不要部分を筆で取り除き、また吹いては取り除く。電気炉に入れて焼き付ける。それを繰り返します。

焼き付け回数は、通常5〜6回のところ、本作3点では特に多くて8回となりました。筆で描いたら早そう？ しかし、吹き付けた点と点が並置され、さらに焼き付けによって層を幾重にも成している、そうしたことが光の量と到達のタイミングをコントロールしながら網膜に働きかける効果はほかに換えられません。絵であり物語でありオブジェクトである、すべてを規定する光の企みに心が揺さぶられます。

Traveling

Until now, Ikemoto Kazumi had hardly even touched a handheld game console. *Pokémon Sword and Pokémon Shield*, which he just acquired, is, Ikemoto says, the first video game he has experienced. With the commission for creating a related work, he was able to receive reference materials, including information on the requested scene and details about Pokémon. We thought that might be enough for him, when confirming the information he needed. “No, that’s no good.” Come to think of it, Ikemoto had written earlier, about creating glass, “Knowing how I sense the subject is vitally important when making a drawing.” His long period of game play, until he finally reached the *Hall of Fame*, was time to look, feel, and think, using a game console instead of pen, pencil, or brush. The “experience” sought in a fictional universe was a process during which Pokémon and Ikemoto Kazumi, the artist, fused their world views.

The setting of this work is the Galar region. The Pokémon Trainer boy and his partners—the Pokémon Ikemoto selected while playing—have all sorts of adventures while traveling from Postwick to Wyndon. The three-dimensional picture scroll, in three parts, Ikemoto created includes landmarks deeply familiar to Pokémon fans. These depictions of landscapes, so characteristic of Ikemoto, develop as a series, inviting one to an as-yet-unseen future.

Light, Light, Light,

The rich colors celebrate memories of the journey. Ikemoto used red, yellow, three greens, two blues, and pale orange, a total of eight colors. Those colors—achieved using his enamel technique—are so varied and vivid that one is tempted to ask, “Just eight colors?” Enamels are materials prepared to apply metal compounds to glass, then fired at a low temperature to fuse them to the glass. Ikemoto dissolves enamel pigments in alcohol and blows them on glass. He blows each color separately, uses a brush to remove any excess pigments, blows again, and removes again. He then places the work in an electric kiln, to fuse the enamels to the glass. He repeats those processes over and over.

Usually he fires a work five to six times, but he used eight firings, a particularly large number, in creating these three pieces. Wouldn’t it be faster just to paint with a brush? But with his tech-

❶「エナメル」材料と道具
❷ 霧吹きの作業｜1色ずつ作業する。アルコールが蒸発するとガラスに粉が乗っただけの状態なので、さわるとすぐに取れてしまう。トップと底しか手の置きどころがない25kgのボディを電気炉に入れるのも一苦労。
❸ 1回目絵付け｜《冒険のはじまり》(p.56別アングル)｜紫系の青単色で、陰影や細部まで描きこまれている様子がうかがえる。デッサンのような感じで、このプロセスが一番時間がかかる。
❹ 3回目焼き付け｜《殿堂入り》(p.58別アングル)

❶ Materials and tools for enamelling
❷ Blowing | The process is carried out one color at a time. When the alcohol evaporates, only the pigment particles are on the glass, which means they can be removed right away, just by touching them. Putting the 25-kilogram body of this work in the kiln, when the body can only be held at the top and bottom, is a difficult step.
❸ First decoration: *Adventure Begins* (another angle from p.56) | We can see even shadows and details depicted in the purplish-blue pigment. This stage seems like a design drawing and is the process that takes the longest time.
❹ Third firing: *Hall of Fame* (another angle from p.58)

nique, the spots of enamel are placed side by side and then made into multiple layers, thanks to the firing. It is a technique that is irreplaceable, since it allows Ikemoto to control the amount of light and the timing of its arrival while working on our retinas. A painting, a narrative, an object: all his works, with their scheme of strictly controlled light, stir our hearts.

林茂樹　Hayashi Shigeki

月光 Pokémon Edition |
"Moonlight" Pokémon Edition

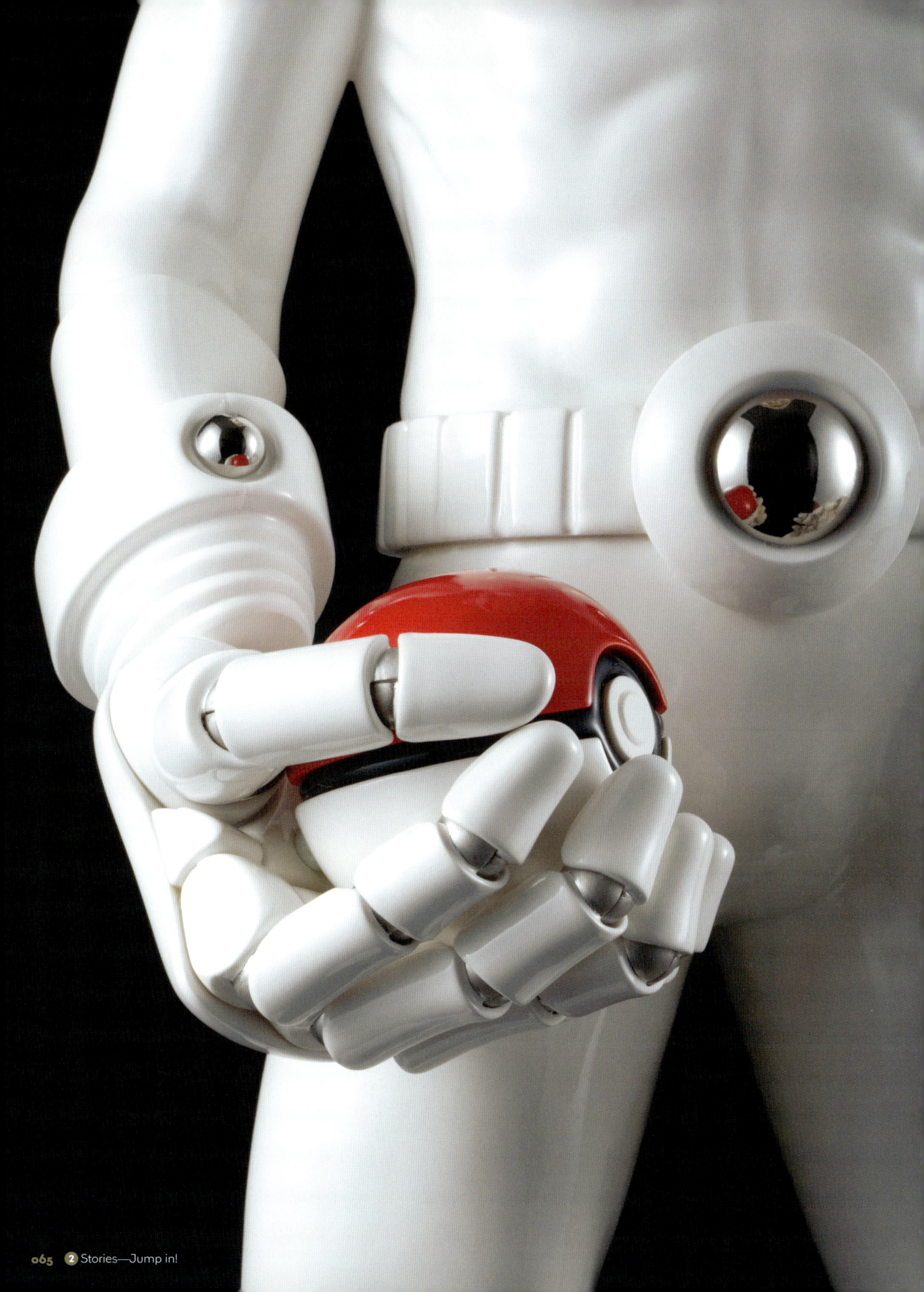

林茂樹
Hayashi Shigeki

遊び

林茂樹は、自身の作品が「国や文化、世代を超えた世界共通言語」となることを理想に掲げてきました。今日、ポケモンは地域や言語、年齢層を超えて世界的な人気を博しています。そのことに強い興味をもった林は「文化的背景を越えた共有可能な普遍的価値」の在処に思いをめぐらせます。しかし、異なるヴィジョンをひとつの作品に共存させるのは容易ではありません。さんざん悩んだ挙句、彼が到達したのは“遊び”という視点でした。オランダの歴史学者、J.ホイジンガが提唱した「ホモ・ルーデンス」の概念にもあるとおり、遊びは人の生の営みの根源であり、文化を生み、推進する力ともなります。さらに林は日本語の遊びに“余白”の意を重ねましたが、これもまた鋭い眼識であり、私たちが今回の作品の魅力を味わうための重要なカギをもたらしました。

身体をぴったりと覆い、優れた性能を予感させる数々の装備。《月光 Pokémon Edition》の出で立ちは、ポケモンの世界に向けて林が仕掛けた「遊びゴコロ」の結晶です。ポケモントレーナーがこのスペシャルなスーツを着用したならば……。想像力のリミッターはここで完全に解放。表層に光が走り、遊びの出力も最大に上げられるに違いありません。豊かな頬の子どもは無限の可能性の象徴。抑制された表情の奥で静かな笑みを湛え、視線の先に私たちを誘います。マフラーをたなびかせるのは、広大なフィールドに吹き抜ける風でしょうか。繊細な指の仕草。モンスターボールの赤が冴え、目を惹きつけてまた掻き立てられる。果たしてこの子の次のアクションやいかに。細部各処を徹底してこだわり抜きながら、心を寄せる余地を設けたのもさすがの采配です。純白の輝きを前にした鑑賞者の数だけ、想像の世界が広がります。

磁器：焼物の一種で素地は白色。透光性があり、吸水性はない。長石・カオリン・珪石などの鉱物を砕いて粘土状に練ったものを主原料とするため、石物とも呼ばれる。焼成温度は焼物のなかで最も高く、一次焼成の際には1400°Cを超えることもある。素焼したあと、釉薬を施して再び焼き上げる。素地・釉ともにガラス化が進んでいるため陶器に比べて硬く、指で軽くはじくと金属のような音を発する。

Play

Hayashi Shigeki has always held the ideal that his work would become “a global common language, one that transcends country, culture, or period.” Pokémon has achieved the global pop-

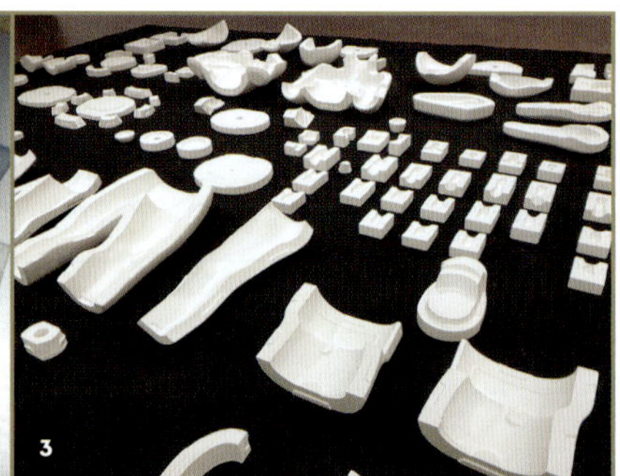

❶粘土原型から石膏で型（捨て型）を取り、石膏を流し入れ、石膏原型を作る。粘土では限界のある表面処理も石膏ではミリ以下の精度が可能となる。
❷石膏原型をもとに再び石膏で鋳込用本型を制作。型の割り線を決めたあと、不要部分を粘土で埋め、壁を立て、順番に型を取る。
❸石膏型の総数は130以上。1つのパーツにつき2〜3個割が基本だが、ベルトのように10個割のものもある。

❶ Hayashi makes a plaster of paris mold from the clay model, fills it with plaster of paris, and creates the plaster of paris model. The surface treatment, which is limited with clay, can be carried out at the millimeter or less level with plaster of paris.
❷ Using the plaster of paris models, the molds for casting are made of plaster of paris. After deciding where the molds will be split, the unnecessary parts are filled with clay, making walls, and the casting proceeds, piece by piece.
❸ There are more than 130 plaster of paris molds. Basically one part is divided into two or three molds, but pieces like the belt use ten.

❹ 鋳込み｜泥漿（磁器土を液体状に調整したもの）を型に流し込み、石膏の吸水性を利用して成形する。パーツのサイズごとに必要な肉厚が違うため、時間を変え余分な泥漿を排泥する。
❺ 乾燥後、型から外したパーツを丁寧に成形し、さらに時間をかけて乾燥させる。今回のパーツは104個。800°Cで素焼したあと、表面を耐水ペーパーなどで磨いて仕上げる。釉薬をかけたくない部分に撥水処理を施し、乳白釉を施釉。

❹ Casting | Slip (porcelain clay treated so that it becomes liquid) is poured into the mold. The plaster of paris's water absorbency is used form the piece. Since the thickness needed for each of the parts differs, depending on the size, the time for casting them varies. Excess slip will be poured out.
❺ After they dry, the parts removed from the molds are carefully formed and allowed to dry longer. This work consisted of 104 parts. After bisque firing at 800°C, the surfaces were polished with waterproof paper or other materials. Areas to be left unglazed were waterproofed, then milky white glaze applied.

ularity, spanning borders, languages, and age groups. Strongly interested in that development, Hayashi pondered “universal values that can be shared, overcoming cultural backgrounds.“ It is not, however, easy to have different visions coexisting in one work. After many struggles, he arrived at “play” as his viewpoint. According to the concept of “homo ludens” proposed by the Dutch historian Johan Huizinga, play is the foundation of human activity, creating and promoting culture. In addition, Hayashi overlaps the meaning of play with the Japanese term *yohaku* (blank space), a keen insight that provides us with a valuable key to experiencing the fascination of this work.

All sorts of equipment to cover the body perfectly and give a sense of outstanding capabilities. The outfit of the *“Moonlight” Pokémon Edition* is the fruit of the playfulness that Hayashi directed at the Pokémon world. Upon seeing this special suit, Pokémon Trainers are free to imagine themselves wearing it ... and what the possibilities might be. Light runs across the surface, and the output of playfulness must be boosted to the max. A plump-cheeked child is a symbol with unlimited possibilities. The expression is restrained but filled with a quiet smile, inviting us to share his gaze. Is it the wind blowing across the vast field that makes the mufflers flutter? The delicate positioning of the fingers. The red of the Poké Ball is gleaming, attracting our eyes and stirring us up. What will this child's next action be? Hayashi has taken great care with the fine details, yet also, as we would expect from him, has reserved the *yohaku* he cares so much about. Worlds of imagination open up, one for every viewer who stands before this pure white glow!

❻ 施釉後、タレなどを削り、表面をムラのない均一な状態にする。16時間かけて1230℃で焼成。1度でうまくいかない場合が多く、焼き直す。プラチナ彩を800℃で焼き付け。パーツは接着剤やボルトなどで組み立て。これらの丹念なプロセスを経て、柔らかそうな子供の皮膚から白く輝く未来的な装備まで、すべてに磁器がもつ素材の魅力と美しさが息づいた。

❻ After applying the glaze, drips and other imperfections are removed so that the surfaces are completely even. The parts are then fired for sixteen hours at 1230°C. If that firing is insufficient, which is often the case, those parts are fired again. Platinum pigment is applied and fired at 800°C. The parts are assembled using glue and bolts. Through this elaborate process, the beauty and charm of porcelain radiates through everything, from the soft-seeming child-like skin to the futuristic equipment with its white glow.

•

Porcelain: A kind of pottery with a white body, usually translucent and impervious to water. Because key materials include minerals such as feldspar, kaolin and silica, which are crushed and kneaded into clay, it is also referred to in Japanese as *ishimono* (stone material). The firing temperature is the highest for pottery, with primary firing at sometimes over 1,400°C. After the bisque firing, it is glazed and fired again. As both base and glaze are quite vitrified, porcelain is harder than stoneware. It sounds metallic when lightly struck.

坪島悠貴　Tsuboshima Yuki

可変金物 ココガラ／アーマーガア |
Transformable Ornament, Rookidee / Corviknight

坪島悠貴

Tsuboshima Yuki

可変金物

金属製の小さなオブジェクトで、パーツを動かすと姿かたちが異なるモチーフに変わります。機構・名称ともに坪島悠貴自身が考案。今回は1つの可変金物に**ココガラ**と**アーマーガア**の2匹のポケモンが共生しました。

インターネットで見かけて以来、アーマーガアは、坪島にはたまらなくカッコイイ存在でした。一方のココガラは、参考にプレイした『ポケットモンスター ソード・シールド』ですぐに捕まえられたことりポケモン。「可愛いなぁ」と調べると、進化の線上にアーマーガアを発見。「こんな可愛いやつが、(アオガラスを経て)アーマーガアに進化するんだとびっくり」して、この2種での制作を決めました。

子どもの頃からカラスに対して深い思い入れをもっていた坪島は、アーマーガアも「翼の大きさ、迫力を強調したい」と考え、この堂々たる姿となるように設計しました。ココガラには手で包み込めるコロッとしたフォルムのなかに「勇敢で　向こう見ずな　気質」をにじませたのも楽しい対比です。ポケモンでは進化は一方向ですが、可変金物はカワイイ⇄カッコイイが自在。ポケモンと作家のイメージの交錯がこの小さなオブジェクトへの興味の深化を促します。

最適解

坪島が可変金物に取り組むきっかけとなったのは「根付」。根付は留め具の1種で、煙草入れや印籠などを帯から吊るすために用います。それまでの坪島は、打ち出しという金工の技で、生きものの姿を金属板から立体成形していました。が、根付となれば携行品の荷重に耐えて揺れ、また身に着け、外すアクションの想定も求められます。破損や衣服への引っかけ回避のために考えたのが「細かいパーツを全部収納」作戦で、それが造形に変形パターンの論理を取り入れた始まりでした。

坪島の仕事は複雑な仕掛けの面白さもさることながら、それを実現する個々のパーツと機構とが必然によって導き出されているのも見どころです。50数パーツで構築された《可変金物 ココガラ／アーマーガア》の小さなボディには、工芸を考えるさまざまなヒントが隠れていそうです。

❶こんな「感じ」メモ。「したい」仕組みの内容。パーツ形状や組み合わせの角度、動かし方。各段階でさまざまに検討。
❷「ココガラ」試作｜詳細データ制作の前のラフなモデル。

❶ Memo of "this sort of feel." In contains the contraption he wants to create, plus the shapes of the parts, the angles at which they fit together, and how they move. Tsuboshima was considering various things at each stage.
❷ Trial version of *Rookidee* | Rough model before producing detailed data.

ココガラ
Rookidee

アーマーガア
Corviknight

3

4

5

6

❸3D CADデータ①|頭のなかのイメージが現実に成立するのか検証。物理的な制約によっては再考もあるが、ココガラ腹部の曲面とアーマーガアの肩の反り返り部分を表裏一体とするのは最初からのアイディア。
❹3D CADデータ②|このあと3Dプリンタで原型出力→各パーツをシリコンで型取り→シリコン型に専用のワックスを注入→シリコンから取り出したワックスを石膏に埋没→焼成→ワックスが消える→石膏型に熔かした金属を入れて成形、と続く。
❺色合い最終調整|ココガラの目は電着塗装を計画。焼き付けるので強い塗膜を得られる。貴石のような輝きは「下地をめちゃくちゃ磨いてある」。コンピュータの使用と、その合間に坪島自身が手で行う調整・仕上げ作業。あらゆることが作品の精確と正確のために放つ技である。
❻組み立て|前の姿を変形後の外殻が覆う構造。「パーツの間から見える内部構造みたいなものにグッとくる感覚が昔からあった」。このあと着彩。

❸ 3D CAD data ① | Checking whether the image he had thought of is realized. Rethinking happens due to physical limitations, but the curved surface of Rookidee's chest and the backwards bend of Corviknight's upper wings were planned to be inextricably linked from the start.
❹ 3D CAD data ② | Next he outputs the model with a 3D printer, makes silicon molds from it, fills the silicon molds with a special type of wax, removes the wax from the silicon, covers the wax in gypsum, bakes it so that the wax melts away, pours liquified metal in the gypsum mold, and forms the metal part.
❺ Final adjustment of coloring | The plan was to use electrodeposition for Rookidee's eyes. The color would be fired on, for a strong layer of paint. The gem-like glitter is from "polishing the ground like mad." The work uses a computer and also, between steps, Tsuboshima adjusting and finishing by hand. All the techniques are used to ensure the work's precision and accuracy.
❻ Assembly | The structure with the exterior shell covering it after transformation from the previous form. "I've always been touched when I see the internal structure between the parts." And then applying color.

•

Transformable Ornament

A small metallic object that can change its form to another motif, by moving its parts. Both the mechanism and the Japanese name for it were conceived by Tsuboshima Yuki himself. Here two Pokémon, **Rookidee** and **Corviknight**, are coexisting on one transformable ornament.

Since glimpsing Corviknight on the internet, Tsuboshima has found it tremendously cool. Rookidee is the Tiny Bird Pokémon that, while Tsuboshima was playing *Pokémon Sword and Pokémon Shield* for reference, he caught immediately. Examining it, thinking, "How cute!" Tsuboshima discovered Corviknight further up the Evolutionary line. "It's amazing that this cute critter could, after its stage as Corvisquire evolve into Corviknight!" He thus decided to create a work combining both of them.

Tsuboshima had been deeply interested in crows since childhood and thought, for Corviknight, "I want to emphasize the size of the wings and their power." He designed it to have this imposing appearance. Rookidee's form, small enough to hold in the palm of your hand, reveals "a brave and reckless character." The contrast between the two is delightful. A Pokémon's Evolution is unidirectional, but this transformable object can be cute or cool, at will. The intersection between Pokémon and the artist's imagination makes this tiny object even more intriguing.

•

An Optimal Solution

It was *netsuke* that inspired Tsuboshima to work on transformable ornaments. A *netsuke* is a type of fastener, usually a small sculpture, used when hanging a tobacco pouch or an *inro* (a tiered container) from the *obi* sash. Until then, Tsuboshima had created three-dimensional forms of living things using metal sheets and the hammering technique. A *netsuke*, however, has to bear the weight of the portable object it is fastening, while swinging. And it also requires the assumption that, as an accessory worn on the body, it can be attached and removed. To avoid damage and parts getting snared on clothing, he decided that "all the fine parts should be put inside," and took up the challenge. That was the start of incorporating that form in the logic of his transformative patterns.

Tsuboshima's work is of course intriguing for its intricacies, but the way that the individual parts and mechanisms are needed to work is also fascinating. The small body of *Transformable Ornament, Rookidee/Corviknight* is made of fifty-some parts. It conceals all sorts of suggestions for thinking about the craft.

城間栄市　Shiroma Eiichi

琉球紅型着物「島ツナギ」｜
Kimono “Island to Island,” Ryukyu *Bingata*

琉球藍型着物「島ツナギ」|
Kimono, “Island to Island,” Ryukyu *Egata*

城間栄市
Shiroma Eiichi

紅型

沖縄で行われる型染で、城間家は紅型三宗家の1つ。16代目を継承するにあたり、城間栄市は紅型の再定義を試みました。しばしば県外の人から言われ、自身も感じていた紅型の「豊かさ」「沖縄らしさ」とはなんだろう。多彩で、明るい。おおどかだが底が深く、組み合わせの妙が開く可能性は無尽とも見える。そして城間が辿り着いた「生み出す島」というヴィジョンは、紅型に親しむためのキーワードとなりそうです。

今回、城間は制作のイメージに、ポケモン原作の舞台の1つである南国の「アローラ地方」を重ねました。アダンの葉4枚を1単位とするパターンにやってきたポケモンは**ピカチュウ**、**ライチュウ**、**モクロー**、**ニャビー**、**アシマリ**、そして4つの島それぞれに棲む**オドリドリたち**。紅型の5色（赤、青、黄、緑、ピンク）がみごとにはまりました。紅型特有の、濃い色でアクセントをつける隈取の効果にも注目。ポケモンたちの生き生きとした存在感がいや増し、アダンを揺らす風に乗って飛び出していきそうです。

藍型

紅型との大きな違いは浸染であること。型附後、青系顔料の濃淡を筆で挿し、隈取までやってから、城間家では着尺用の大甕（口径90cm!）に建てた琉球藍に浸けます。防染糊が染液のなかでゆるむので、キリッとした紅型と比べて染際に柔らかさが出るのも藍型の魅力です。藍染は液に浸けるだけでなく、引き上げるたびに空気中で酸化させることで色を濃くしていきますが、何度も染液をくぐった藍地のなんと味わい深いこと。天然の藍ならではの多様なニュアンスが、化学染料のシャープさとはまた違った豊かさをもたらしました。白く染め抜かれた輪郭や顔は、月光を受けたかのように浮かび上がっていかにも楽しげです。紅型作品と好一対。2点協働して時空を超えた旅に見る人を誘います。

旅

旅はポケモン世界でも重要なエッセンス。初めての土地、そして人やポケモンたちとの出会いが主人公の成長を促します。城間栄市も沖縄の離島、台湾、そしてインドネシアなどを旅しましたが、そうした記憶は「その地に降り立ったときの独特の匂いを運ぶ“風”」に始まるようです。

今回の主題は「旅の風」。植物モチーフが色を変えながら繰り返し配され、吹き抜ける風がワクワク気分を掻き立てました。制作を通してポケモンを“旅”した城間ですが、そこに「仮想現実とも言い切れない、拡張現実に近い感覚」を抱いたのだとか。「たとえば台風を見て紅型を思いつくように、自分たちは景色を工芸として理解して描く。ポケモンの世界にも共通するところがあるのかも」。他者と接して、あらためて自分を発見した様子。これもまた旅の醍醐味かもしれません。

Bingata

The Shiroma family is one of the three main families in Okinawa engaged in traditional *bingata* stenciled resist dyeing, and as the 16th successor, Shiroma Eiichi has endeavored to redefine *bingata*. What is the nature of the richness and quintessential Okinawan-ness of *bingata* that people from outside the prefecture have often commented on, and that he has personally felt? It is colorful and vibrant. It is both generous and deep, and the effect of its combinations open up a seemingly inexhaustible range of patterns. Shiroma has arrived at the vision of a "fertile islands," which seems to be a key concept for deepening one's familiarity with *bingata*.

For this project's imagery, Shiroma drew inspiration from the tropical Alola region, one of the settings in the Pokémon video game series. The Pokémon appearing in the stenciled pattern, in which four leaves of the fragrant screw pine plant form a unit, are **Pikachu**, **Raichu**, **Rowlet**, **Litten**, **Popplio**, and **Oricorio**, the last of which inhabits each of the four islands that make up Alola. The five colors used in *bingata* (red, blue, yellow, green, and pink) fit the motifs splendidly, and the shading effect characteristically used to accentuate dark colors in *bingata* is noteworthy as well. The vigorous presence of the Pokémon is enhanced, and they seem to be soaring outward on the wind that ruffles the screw pines.

Egata

Egata's major difference from *bingata* is that it is a dip-dyeing process. After a stenciled pattern is attached, shades of blue pigment are applied with a brush, and in the Shiroma family, fab-

ピカチュウ
Pikachu

ライチュウ
Raichu

モクロー
Rowlet

ニャビー
Litten

アシマリ
Popplio

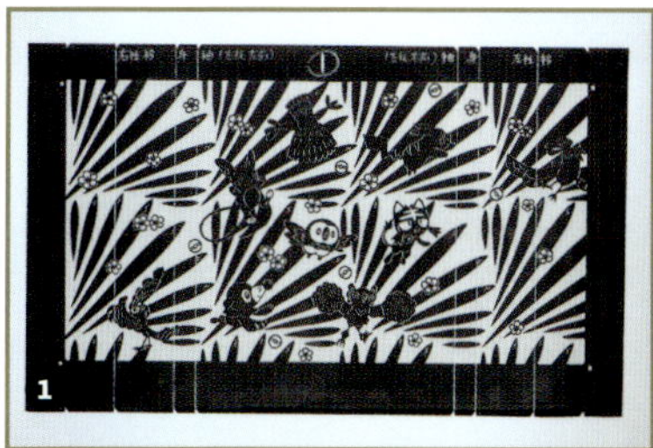

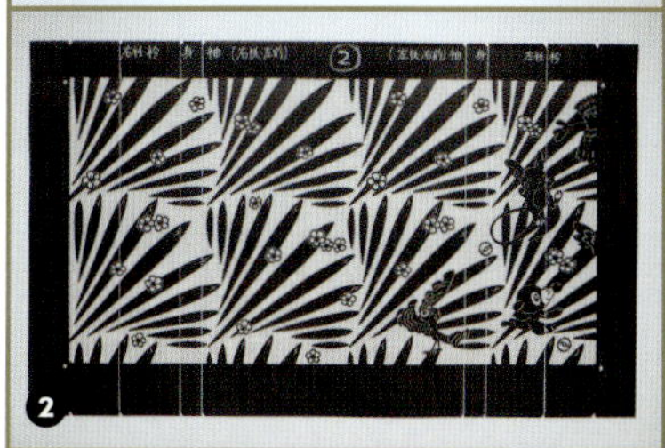

❶ 型紙① | この型紙を用いて型附(生地に型紙を置き防染糊を施す)。その後色挿(モチーフ部分に筆で彩色)→隈取→伏糊(モチーフ部分を糊で覆う)→地染→蒸し(染料を生地にしっかり定着させる)→水元(糊や余分の染料を洗い流す)の手順で紅型の鮮やかな色と模様とが浮かび上がる。
❷ 型紙② | 紅型には①から③の型紙3枚をすべて用いて、①→②→③の順に配列。
❸ 紗張り(型紙③) | 今回の型紙はいずれも余白を生かした構成。バラバラにならないよう、いったんツリ(繋ぎ目)を残した状態で型を彫り上げ、紗(目の粗い織物)を貼ったあと、ツリを切り取る。
❹ 図案

❶ Stencil ① | This stencil is placed on the fabric and resist paste is applied. The subsequent procedure consists of applying color to the motifs with a brush → Shading → Resist application (covering the motifs with paste) → Dyeing of entire fabric → Steaming (to affix the dye firmly to the fabric) → Washing off of glue and excess dye, to reveal the vivid colors and patterns of the finished *bingata*.
❷ Stencil ② | The *bingata* process employs three stencils, used in the appropriate order.
❸ Fabric stretching (stencil ③) | Each of the stencils in this project was composed by making effective use of blank space. To prevent the stenciled patterns from getting out of sync, the stencil is first cut out with the seams remaining, coarse textile is stretched over it, and then the seams are cut out.
❹ Design drawing

ric the length of a kimono is then dipped into a large vassel (90 cm in diameter!) of Ryukyu indigo. The resist paste is loosened in the dye solution, which gives the dyed fabric an appearance softer than that of crisp *bingata*. Indigo dyeing involves not only soaking in solution, but also oxidization in the air each time the fabric is pulled out to darken the color. The multifarious nuances of natural indigo bring forth richness distinct from the sharp effect of chemical dyes. The outlines and faces left in white appear as if they were illuminated by the moonlight and look very happy. *Egata* makes for a delightful contrast with *bingata*, as the two pieces work in harmony to take the viewer on a journey through time and space.

•

Journeys

Embarking on a journey is an essential aspect of the Pokémon universe. Encounters with new places, people, and Pokémon help the protagonist grow. Shiroma Eiichi has gone on various journeys to remote islands in Okinawa, Taiwan, and Indonesia, and he says his memories of these begin with "the wind that carries the unique fragrance of the land when you first arrive."

The theme of this exhibit is "Wind of Journeys." Repeated plant motifs are arrayed in different colors, and the wind that seems to waft through them stirs a sense of excitement. In creating these works Shiroma "journeyed" through Pokémon, and felt "a sense not quite like virtual reality, but more like augmented reality... it was as if we grasped and depicted the landscape in the language of crafts, just as one might see a typhoon and be inspired to create *bingata*. Perhaps there is something similar in the world of Pokémon." The artist seemed to discover a new self through contact with others. This is perhaps one of the greatest joys of a journey.

工房の入口
Studio entrance

オドリドリ(めらめらスタイル)
Baile Style Oricorio

オドリドリ(ぱちぱちスタイル)
Pom-Pom Style Oricorio

オドリドリ(ふらふらスタイル)
Pa'u Style Oricorio

オドリドリ(まいまいスタイル)
Sensu Style Oricorio

須藤玲子　Sudo Reiko

須藤玲子

Sudo Reiko

kawaii

須藤玲子がデザインディレクターを務めるNUNOの布の魅力の1つは発想力の豊かなこと。たとえば、ノートかどこかに貼りついた輪ゴムの跡。あるいは手持ち無沙汰のうちに折りたたんだ紙のしわ。そうした何気ない日常のひとコマにもテキスタイルの芽が見いだされます。本展の初顔合わせでも須藤のセンサーは鋭く、素早くフル回転。「ポケモンは息子と一緒にアニメを見たくらいで、あまり知らないのだけれど」とためらいながら、しかし「ポケモンずかん」で目に留まったポケモンを次々と観察。そのグラフィカルな特徴、そこに技やタイプなども加味して、さまざまな"ポケモン×テキスタイル"のイメージを織り成していきました。

そして最終的に決まったモチーフは「すごく可愛い、可愛くて気になる」と須藤が繰り返し眺めていた**ピカチュウ**。別のポケモンで素材技法から展示プランまで組み上がった案も出たのですが、「でもやっぱり可愛い」ピカチュウの魅力をテキスタイルで語りたい思いに突き動かされたのです。モチーフの語源はラテン語の「motivus(動かす)」。「可愛い」熱は制作に携わった関係者に広がって、ともに作品のクオリティ向上を目指す力となったようです。

[左]原画|植物モチーフの検討
[右]切り絵イメージ
[left] Design drawing exploring vegetative motifs
[right] Decorative cut-paper version

チームワーク

約900本の"ピカチュウレース"で構成した今回の出品作は、題名が示すとおり、アニメ「ポケットモンスター」の「ピカチュウのもり」にインスピレーションを得ました。1点モノの貴重性に心からの敬意を抱くその一方で、美しく、楽しいもののリピートに強く惹かれる須藤です。だからこそ量産を前提とするデザインの現場に立つわけですが、そんな須藤にとって「もり」は、直感を実証するのにぴったりな題材だったといえます。

手法はNUNOが80年代末から作り続けているニードルレース。まずは個々のモチーフをノートに描きだします。ピカチュウの棲息地にはどんな植物が生える/映えるだろうかと考えたのが、原始的な生命力を感じさせる羊歯やツル草、ゼンマイ、キノコ。高山植物は可憐な姿で文字通り花を添え、山ごとに固有種に分化する傾向も特別な場にふさわしいセレクトでした。原画の線描を切り絵で面に置換してバランスを確認。ここまではNUNOのアトリエで。その後、バトンを工場に渡してドット絵で作画。

糸の密度が決まったら石灰を原料とする布シートに機械でステッチし、それを水洗いするとシートが溶けて繊細なレースのリボンが残ります。各モチーフのシルエットは一筆書きで行き来するステッチ糸で描出しますが、聞けば糸の軌跡の詳細は工場に委ねるのだとか。「自分1人ではなくいろいろな職能の方との協働」は、互いの意を汲み、専門の技を尽くして1人では到達しなかったかもしれない先に突き進むこと。そこに須藤はデザインの醍醐味を感じます。

さあ、糸の物質感と光のグラデーションで満たされたテキスタイル空間が開かれました。1本だけ色柄違いのレースがあります。主題の決め手となった、川に落ちたピカチュウを仲間のピカチュウが助ける「最高に可愛い」姿をデザインです。お見逃しなく。

Kawaii

Among the charms of fabrics produced by NUNO, of which Sudo Reiko is design director, is their abundance of imagination. For example, the germination of their textile designs can be found in trivial everyday occurrences, such as a rubber band sticking to a notebook or something and making a mark, or the creases in a

ピカチュウ
Pikachu

piece of paper folded in an idle moment. During our first meeting to discuss this exhibition, Sudo's sensors were on full alert, and she was fully engaged with the project immediately. While she said hesitantly at first, "I don't know much about *Pokémon* outside of watching the anime with my son," she made many keen observations about Pokémon that caught her eye in the Pokédex. She noted the visual characteristics of various species and their unique moves and types, and succeeded in weaving together a variety of images for "Pokémon x Textiles."

The motif eventually decided upon was **Pikachu**, which Sudo had repeatedly seen and admired as "so *kawaii* [cute], really adorable." While proposals for other Pokémon motifs were drawn up, from material and technique to exhibition plan, Sudo was motivated by the desire to convey the appeal of Pikachu through textiles: "After all, it's so *kawaii*!" Incidentally, the word "motif" is etymologically derived from the Latin *motivus* (to move). *Kawaii* fever seems to have spread to everyone involved in the production, and helped propel their motivation to maximize the quality of the work.

•

Teamwork

The exhibit consists of approximately 900 ribbons of "Pikachu lace," which was inspired by one of Pikachu's adventures in a forest in the Pokémon television animation series. While having the sincerest reverence for the preciousness of one-of-a-kind items, Sudo is also strongly drawn to the repetition of what is beautiful and delightful. That is why she works in the field of mass-produced design, and a forest was the perfect subject for her to put her intuitions to work.

The technique is needle lace, which NUNO has been making since the late 1980s. She began by drawing individual motifs in her notebook. She thought about what kinds of plants would grow or appear in Pikachu's habitat: ferns, vines, fronds, and mushrooms evoke primitive vitality. Dainty alpine plants literally added to the flowering of the design, and their tendency to differentiate into species endemic to individual mountains also made them an appropriate selection for this special project. The original line drawings were turned into two-dimensional forms using *kiri-e* (decorative paper cutting) to ascertain their balance. Work up to this point was done in the NUNO studio, and then it was handed off to the factory where pixel art was created.

Once thread density was determined, the design was machine-stitched onto a sheet of fabric derived from lime, which was then rinsed in water, dissolving the sheet and leaving only delicate lace ribbon. The silhouettes of each motif were rendered with stitches that go back and forth in a single line, but according to Sudo, the details of the thread's path are left to the factory. She says that "collaborating with people of various skilled trades rather than working alone" allows people to draw on one another's expertise and reach a destination they might not have been able to reach on their own. It is in this process that Sudo finds the true joy of design.

The result is an expansive textile space filled with the materiality of threads and gradations of light. Only one of the lace ribbons has a different color and pattern. Its design depicts "the cutest Pikachu ever" in the act of rescuing one of its comrades from falling into the river, a scene that was the decisive factor in selecting this motif. Don't miss it!

1

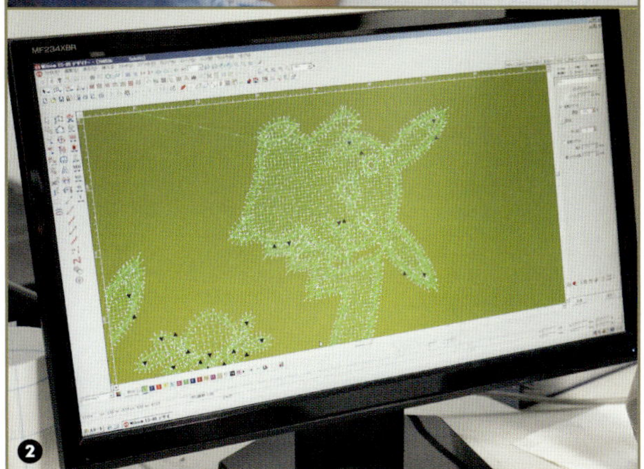

2

3

❶ドット絵
❷データ調整
❸テスト機
❶ Pixel art
❷ Data conditioning
❸ Embroidery prototype

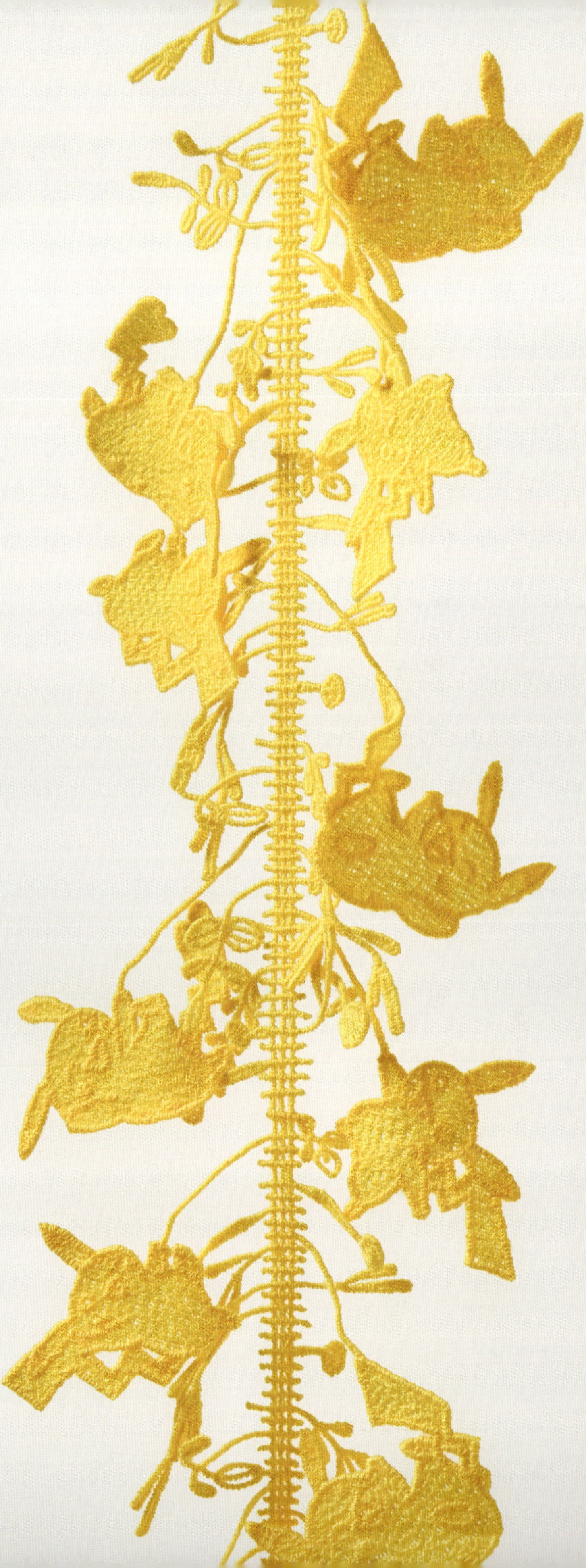

Life — Cherish!

3 くらし — 愛でる!

工芸は生活のさまざまなシーンをより良く、美しく整え、活力を与えてくれるものです。その機能や装飾の文法と価値観に、ここではポケモンが挑戦しました。壺と一緒に高温の炎を体験したり、季節の訪れを知らせたり、整然と並びながらしなやかな絹地のうえで踊ってみたりと大健闘。器や着物、装身具を舞台に活躍するポケモンたちのなんと楽しげなこと。その様子を目で追いかけるうちに、皆さんのなかにある日々を慈しむ感性がますます豊かになるかもしれません。

Craft can enhance, beautify, and energize many aspects of our lives. Pokémon challenged the etiquette and values of craft's functions and decoration. They put up a good fight to experience hot flames in the kiln with jars, to signal the arrival of the seasons, or to dance on the supple silk fabric while lining up in an orderly fashion. How delightful are the Pokémon that are active on the stage as vessels, kimonos, and ornaments. As you follow them with your eyes, you may find that your sensibility to cherish each and every day becomes even richer.

桂盛仁　Katsura Morihito

[上]香合 ルギア |
[top] Incense Container, Lugia Design
[下]香合 ホウオウ |
[bottom] Incense Container, Ho-Oh Design

［上］帯留 ブラッキー「威嚇」｜
[top] Sash Clasp in Umbreon Shape, "Intimidating"
［中］ブローチ ブラッキー「眠り」｜
[middle] Brooch in Umbreon Shape, "Sleep"
［下］帯留 ブラッキー「立ち姿」｜
[bottom] Sash Clasp in Umbreon Shape, "Standing"

金工
Metal Works

桂盛仁
Katsura Morihito

金具
桂盛仁が「彫金」で重要無形文化財保持者(人間国宝)に認定されるにあたり、特に高く評価されたのが金具の制作です。モチーフ本来の奥行を圧縮し、装飾品に適した新たな奥行感を検討。なだらかな山型に膨らませた地金を鏨で打ち、高いところから低いところへと造形していきます。細部の表情や装飾も同時進行。金具には彫金技法のすべてがある。これは装剣金工「柳川派」の伝統を受け継ぐ父・桂盛行による、まさに至言。

さて、銀の裏板が付けば帯留の完成。わずかに覗く銀が丸みを帯びたフォルムを引き締める輪郭ともなりました。「お! と気づいたときに周縁にヒューッと光る線が走ってグッとくる。それを出すのが最後の仕事」。父から伝えられた日本的な美の粋がそこにあります。

赤銅
銅と金の合金。薬液で煮る(煮色仕上げ)と化学反応が起きて、烏の濡れ羽色とも称えられる黒色を呈します。本展では、この赤銅をボディとするブラッキー"金具"が登場しました。

ブラッキーのために桂盛仁が選んだ金の含有量は「絶対的に5%!」。赤銅の色調は煮色仕上げで形成された被膜内の金の粒子に光が当たることで決まりますが、5%となると「黒に紫が入り、その紫が一段と明るくワーーッて来る」のだとか。

黒一字では語り尽くせない魅力を引き出す微細なるものと光の因子。月の光でイーブイの遺伝子が変化したという、ブラッキー誕生の様子を重ねたくなります。

スケッチ | 「ホウオウ」「ルギア」| 対にすることでポーズや位置の呼応関係が自ずと検討される。それもまた日本的な美意識の現れか。
Sketch: *Ho-Oh* and *Lugia* | It was Katsura's idea of treating the two creatures as a pair and positioning them as though reacting to each other. Here too we see a Japanese aesthetic in action.

香合
茶室で焚くお香を入れる小さな容器。中のお香が取り出されたあとは、「拝見」の声とともに客の手から手をめぐって亭主の心を伝えます。ホウオウとルギアはどちらも「ひこう」タイプですから、香りのおもてなしにぴったりなモチーフ選択ではないでしょうか。

紋金はそれぞれ金と銀のみとし、ホウオウの7色の翼も鏨仕事による光のニュアンスで描写。資料を開いた瞬間、琳派の風神雷神図を思い出したという呼応するパワーが2作品揃ったことで増幅し、象徴性もことさら高く見えるようです。

彫金: 金工技法の一種。金属素地の表面を鏨などを用いて、線や模様を彫ったり、透かしたり、打ち出したり、また切断して造形や装飾をする。別の金属を嵌め込む象嵌も行われる。

ブラッキーの金の輪模様は二重象嵌。赤銅のボディに楕円形の穴を彫って金を嵌め、そこにまた穴を開けて赤銅を象嵌した。香合のホウオウとルギアでも、富山県・高岡で鋳造した唐金(銅と錫を主体とする合金)のボディに金と銀でそれぞれ象嵌されている。

Decorative Metal Fittings
When Katsura Morihito was designated a holder of an Important Intangible Cultural Property (Living National Treasure) for *chokin* (metal engraving), the decorative metal fittings he created were particularly highly regarded. In making them, he considered compressing the depth that the motif would naturally have, to find a new sense of depth suitable for decorative objects. Hammering the base metal, made to bulge in a gentle mountain shape, with his chisel he forms it from high places to low places. The expression of details and decoration proceed at the same time. As

イーブイ
Eevee

ブラッキー
Umbreon

ルギア
Lugia

ホウオウ
Ho-Oh

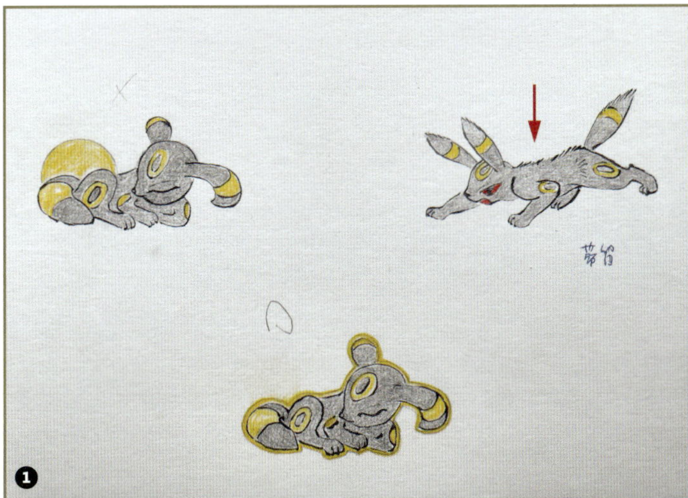

1

2

❶スケッチ｜「眠り」(左、下)と「威嚇」(右)｜「眠り」では月光をどう表すかにも挑戦。試行錯誤の結果、金の裏板を多くとり、柔らかな反射光をまとわせることとなった。
「威嚇」では背中の毛を立たせた。内面の感情を発散してみたいという自身の思いも反映した。
❷粘土原型｜スケッチでポーズや表情を決めたあとのプロセス。「ポトンと垂れて落ちた水滴」の中に納まるように検討する。最も高い(厚みがある)ところから板の際まで、どこから見ても自然な丸みが感じられる。

❶ Sketch: *Sleeping* (left and bottom) and *Intimidating* (right) | For *Sleeping*, the challenge was how to express the moonlight. After some experimentation, Katsura decided on using a lot of gold backplate, to bring together soft reflected light. In the *Intimidating* metal fitting, the fur is standing up on Umbreon's back. That also reflected Katsura's own wish to try to let out his internal sensations.
❷ Clay Models | Creating them is the step in the process after deciding on the pose and expression with the sketches. He considered having the forms fit inside "a drop of water that plopped down." Seen from any point, from the highest part (the thickest) to the edge of the board, the model gives off a sense of natural roundness.

his father, Katsura Moriyuki, who carried on the tradition of the Yanagawa school of metalwork for sword decoration, said, metal fittings, require full mastery of all aspects of engraving techniques. There's much truth in what he said.

Now, he just attached the silver backplate and the *obidome* (sash clasp) is complete. The silver, only slightly visible, has become a contour line pulling together the rounded form. "When someone notices that, rays of light might be racing along the perimeter, which is so exciting. Creating that effect is the last task." Here we find the essence of the Japanese sense of beauty, handed down by his father.

•

Shakudo

A copper and gold, amalgam, when simmered in a chemical solution, a chemical reaction occurs, and the metal acquires a glossy blackish hue. This exhibition includes **Umbreon**-shaped "metal fittings" with *shakudo* body.

For Umbreon, Katsura Morihito said that the gold content would be "Five percent, absolutely!" The blackish-purple tones that the *shakudo* copper amalgam produces result from the action of light on the gold particles in the layer formed on its surface during the chemical reaction. With five percent gold, "Purple joins the black, and that purple is significantly brighter, for a striking effect."

Delicate works that draw out a fascination beyond just plain black, plus the light factor. This play of light may allude to the Evolution of Umbreon from **Eevee** under the light of the moon.

•

Incense Containers

These small containers hold the incense that is burned in a tea room. After the incense is taken out, the guests at the tea ceremony say, "Please let us view it," and hand it from one to another, sharing the host's feelings. Since both **Ho-Oh** and **Lugia** are the "flying" type, they are surely the perfect choice of motif for refreshment with incense, aren't they?

The motif is gold on one and silver on the other, nothing else. The seven colors of Ho-Oh's wings are depicted through the nuance of the light created by his chisel work. At the moment when Katsura saw the reference image of Ho-Oh and Lugia, it reminded him of The Wind God and the Thunder God by Rimpa-school. To make them as a pair, the power of the interaction is amplified and appears to give more emphasis on its symbolism.

•

Metal Engraving: In this type of metalwork, artists use a chisel and other tools applied to the surface of the base metal to carve lines and motifs, create openwork, emboss, and cut it to create forms and decorate them. Inlay is also used, embedding a different metal in the work.

Umbreon's gold ring motifs are dual-layer metal inlay. Katsura carved oval openings in the *shakudo* copper-gold amalgam body and filled them with gold, then opened another space there and applied *shakudo* inlay. The Ho-Oh and Lugia incense containers have bodies of a type of bronze cast in Takaoka, Toyama prefecture, with gold inlay and silver inlay, respectively.

田口義明　Taguchi Yoshiaki

乾漆蒔絵螺鈿蓋物「遊」 |
Lidded Jar, "Play," *Kanshitsu*, *Maki-e* and *Raden* Inlay

蒔絵棗「春を呼ぶ」| Tea Caddy, "Call Spring," *Maki-e*

田口義明
Taguchi Yoshiaki

漆で

今回の展覧会は、「ポケモン」という共通の題材に向かって20名の工芸家の個性が迸(ほとばし)る場。ポケモンのバトルにもなぞらえるユーモアも交えながら、でもすごく真摯に「そこで自分はどう行こうかと考えた」田口義明。自身のタイプは「漆」。あらためて漆とはと尋ねると、次から次へと言葉がこぼれ出ました。しっとりとした艶。手に取ると肌にどこまでも馴染んでやわらかく、視覚で捉えた輪郭とのズレを生じさせ、それが妙なる深みを醸しだす。すぐれた接着剤でもある…。

そうした漆の魅力を最大限に活かすべく、技としたのは「髹漆(きゅうしつ)」と「蒔絵・螺鈿」です。「髹」はこれ一文字で漆を塗るという意味があり、重要無形文化財「髹漆」保持者の増村益城について修得しました。蒔絵・螺鈿の師はいうまでもなく、「蒔絵」で保持者だった父の田口善国です。

蒔絵筆、刷毛｜長い穂先（筆の先）に注目。粘性のある漆を用いても極細の線をスムーズに描ける毛が選ばれる。用具の製作にも熟練の技が求められるが、製作者の廃業が相次ぎ、良質の原料確保が伝統継承の大きな課題となっている。
Maki-e brushes, large and small | Note the long tips of the brushes. The bristles are chosen so that it is possible to draw a smooth, ultra slender line when using *urushi*, which is quite viscous. Producing these tools requires masterful skills, but their makers are going out of business, one after another. Acquiring good quality materials and materials poses a challenge in passing along the traditional skills of *urushi* today.

器物で

《乾漆蒔絵螺鈿蓋物「遊」》に登場したのは**タッツー**、**シードラ**、**キングドラ**。いずれも「みず」タイプのポケモンですから、硬化してもなお、ウェットな印象をもたらす漆と相性の良さは抜群です。肩の張りは胴部のなだらかな曲面へと続きますが、不意打ちのように小さな底部へと切り替わったのにお気づきでしょうか。それがオブジェクト全体に浮遊感をもたらして、渦に乗るタッツーたちと一緒に回遊したくなりそうです。さて造形のバランス的に蓋の摘みは悩みどころ。しかし水指として茶室に置くならば、蓋を片手で持ち上げる所作が求められる。それならば…と蓋の中央に指のかかる穴をうがち、ポケモンたちが巻き起こした渦が中へと流れ込む物語を完成させました。

一方、茶室のスター、棗のモチーフに選んだのは**ファイヤー**です。ボディの主調色には金粉を、頭部や羽から上がる火炎には朱で着色したアルミ粉を蒔いてあります。蒔絵は、器などの表面に漆で絵を描き、粉筒に入れた金属粉を蒔いて付着させる加飾技法です。蒔絵筆で引いた漆の線は直接的には見えませんが、それでも「1本1本が真剣勝負」。これは父の教えのなかでも特に心に刻まれた言葉。ファイヤーが棗の天に振り上げた羽にも気韻生動の美がみなぎり、「春を呼ぶ」使者にふさわしい風格となりました。

In *Urushi* Lacquer

This exhibition is the place where the visions of 20 artists bursts forth as they each uniquely express their style for the subject of Pokémon. But this exciting mission made Taguchi Yoshiaki deeply consider this. "What direction should I go with this subject?" says Taguchi Yoshiaki, wondering how he could capture the humor of a Pokémon Battle. His art medium (or type, to use the Pokémon term), is *urushi* lacquer. Ask him what *urushi* is, and words come tumbling out: Its moist glaze. A surface so smooth that it seems to absorb your touch. The contrast between sight and touch creating a sense of depth. And *urushi* is an excellent adhesive....

The techniques that make the most effective use of *urushi*'s fascination are *kyushitsu*, applying lacquer to a vessel, and *maki-e* and *raden*, sprinkled pictures and mother-of-pearl inlay. The word "*kyu*" by itself can mean applying *urushi*; Taguchi

タッツー
Horsea

シードラ
Seadra

キングドラ
Kingdra

ファイヤー
Moltres

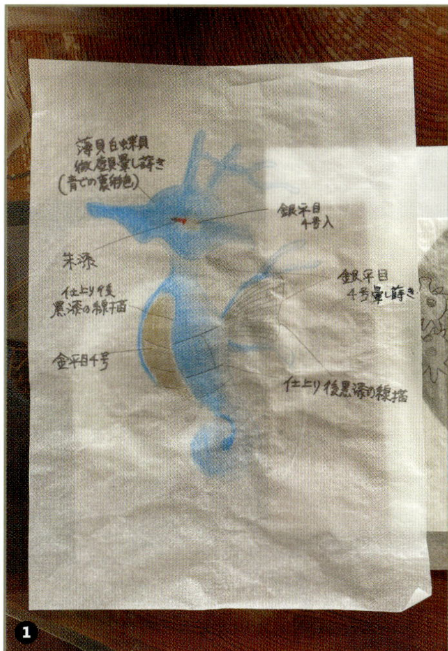

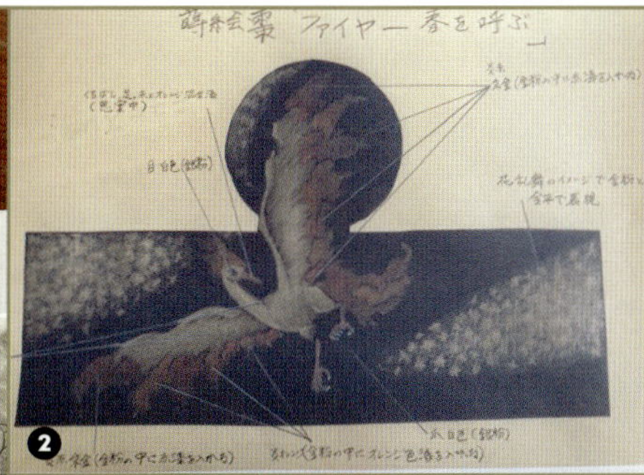

❶図案｜《乾漆蒔絵螺鈿蓋物「遊」》(キングドラ部分)
❷図案｜《蒔絵棗「春を呼ぶ」》
❸図案｜《遊》全体の意匠｜青い部分には着色したアルミ粉を蒔き、その上から白蝶貝の微塵(細かく粉砕したもの)を蒔くプラン。各モチーフ(左からシードラ、タッツー、キングドラ)のサイズや位置とともに、色調や陰影のバランスもここで確認。
❹研ぎ(1回目)｜白蝶貝の微塵を蒔き、漆を塗込んで固めたのち、木炭で研いで貝の輝きを呼び起こす。
❺塗込｜キングドラが薄く透けて見える。研ぎと塗込を繰り返すと、貝の微塵粉を蒔いた部分だけに裏彩色の青が覗く。粉のすき間からこぼれでる漆の艶との対比にも注目したい。

❶ Sketches | Kingdra portion of *Lidded Jar, "Play," Maki-e and Raden inlay*
❷ Sketches | Tea Caddy, *"Calling Spring," Maki-e*
❸ Sketch: Overall design for *Play* | The plan is for the blue area to have colored aluminum powder sprinkled on it, then powdered silver-lipped pearl oyster shell sprinkled above it. Here Taguchi confirmed the size and position of each motif (from the left, Seadra, Horsea, Kingdra) and the balance of colors and shading.
❹ Polishing (first round) | After the powdered silver-lipped pearl oyster shell has been sprinkled, a layer of *urushi* has been applied above it, and the *urushi* has hardened, the piece is polished with charcoal to bring out the shell's glow.
❺ Overcoating | Kingdra appears slightly translucently. Repeated polishings and overcoatings produce the effect in which only the blue of the color applied at the back, on which the fine shell particles were sprinkled, is visible. The contrast with glow of the *urushi* peeking out between the particles is striking.

learned the technique from Masumura Mashiki, who has been designated a holder of an Important Intangible Cultural Property ("Living National Treasure") for *kyushitsu*. Taguchi's instructor in *maki-e* and *raden* was his father, Taguchi Yoshikuni, who was a holder of an Important Intangible Cultural Property ("Living National Treasure") for *maki-e*.

•

With the Vessel Form

The characters who appear in Taguchi's *Lidded Jar, "Play," Kanshitsu, Maki-e and Raden inlay* are **Horsea**, **Seadra**, and **Kingdra**, all Water-type Pokémon. They are unrivaled in the quality they share with *urushi*: continuing to give a wet impression after hardening. The broad shoulders of *Play* continue the gentle curve of the body, but did you notice a slight turning near the bottom, as if it had on a whim? That's part of the floating sensation the artist has given the entire object, as though wanting to make an excursion with Horsea, who rides on a whirlpool. Then, the knob on the lid was a problem in achieving overall balance of form. But if you were to place this work as a fresh-water container in a tea room, it would need a way to lift the lid with one hand. If so.... Taguchi made a hole for a finger to catch in the center of the lid, completing the tale of the Pokémon flowing into it on the whirlpool they generated.

It was **Moltres** that was chosen as the motif for the *natsume* or jujube-shaped tea container, a star in the tea room. Taguchi scattered gold powder on the main color of the body and aluminum powder, colored with vermillion, to the flames rising from head and wings. *Maki-e* is a decoration technique in which a design is drawn in *urushi* on the surface of a vessel or other work and metallic powder is placed in a tube and sprinkled on it, so that it attaches to the still-moist *urushi*. The lines drawn with the *maki-e* brush are not visible directly; it is "a fight in earnest, line by line." That is a phrase Taguchi learned from his father and will never forget. Moltres, fluttering its wings in *natsume's ten* (heaven, the top of the lid of the tea container), is the essence of grace and vitality; and what could be more appropriate for the messenger who signals the arrival of spring?

桑田卓郎 Kuwata Takuro

カップ（ピカチュウ）｜Cups (Pikachu)

陶磁
Ceramics

桑田卓郎
Kuwata Takuro

マイカップ

削ぎ落としたミニマルなボディ。明快な色彩。桑田卓郎の「カップ」シリーズが始まったのは、岐阜県・多治見市陶磁器意匠研究所で学んでいた頃です。生活にもっとも近く、桑田自身がマイカップとして毎日使いたいサイズM。それを現代の基本形としてSとLも加え、今回の展覧会でも3サイズ揃って登場しました。

コアとするフォルムの特徴は、岐阜が誇るマシン量産技術の高さを活かし、手作業では表現できない形を作っています。高さと径のバランスや各部の厚み設定が絶妙に調整され、同時に手取りや口へのあたりのよさも図られました。洗練された意匠のカップは一見工業製品的ですが、1点1点が桑田スタジオのコントロールのもと制作された工芸作品です。

もっともっと

桑田作品のカラーリングはくっきり・明るく・フラット。陶芸に見えないといわれることもある色調ですが、桑田にとっては、これもまた焼きものらしさの体験の1つ。「窯を開けると、あ!となる。もとは水色だったのが、1200°C以上の焼成をくぐり抜け、パッとした真っ青に変化している。その喜び」に感慨を深くし、「もっと」「過剰なほどに」と突き進みました。

早い段階でこの桑田の試みを歓迎したのは、それまで陶芸には親しみがなかった層です。過去の価値観に頼らない「好き」を介した双方向の関心は、桑田の背を押し、また意識を「社会」へと開かせました。「出会いが自分のなかの新たな反応を引き出す。目が向かなかったところに、何かを気づくようになる」。今回の企画ではそのことも「楽しみ」といいます。

桑田が本企画のために選んだモチーフは時代のアイコンである**ピカチュウ**。「現代の最高峰ともいえる岐阜の量産技術を追求しながら制作するカップに配するには、ピカチュウ以外にありえない」とのリスペクトの気持ちがこもっています。リーンなボディは“動力マシン”で成形。ピカチュウの象徴性に匹敵する、現代のスタンダードとしての器物がここで徹底的に精査されました。そしてカラフルな色化粧、ポッテリとした釉薬、金彩とプラチナ彩の輝きで多様性を示し、最後にピカチュウは最新技術による転写シートにて。

最終的に仕上げるまで、焼きものならではの偶発と必然のバランスは困難を極めました。しかしプロセスを重ねるたびにあふれる豊かさは、陶芸事典なしでも、直感的に受けとめられるに違いありません。一方、本作には美濃という窯業地の知識と経験が結集していて、それがこの仕事の骨格でもあります。カップの底から泉のように湧き出るピカチュウの愛らしさに、日本のものづくりの熱意を辿ることができます。

動力成形：石膏型に入れた磁器の粘土を、内ゴテ(棒状の金属)が回転しながら押し込み、型の内壁とコテの回転運動で成形する。内ゴテの当て方で部位ごとに厚みを変えることも可能。

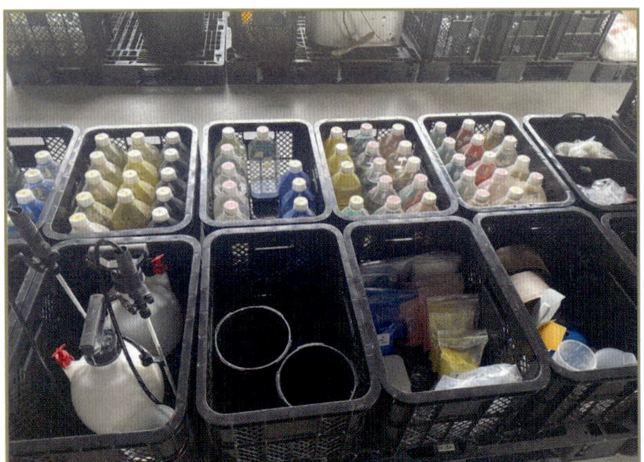

磁器用の土に水を加え、カラフルな顔料を加えて化粧土を作る。素焼した素地にかけて1230°Cで本焼。ボディも色もソリッドに仕上げる。
Making the slip by adding water to the clay used for porcelains and adding colors. The slip is applied to the bisque fired, unglazed works, which are then fired again at 1230 degrees centigrade, in the glost firing, making both the body and colors solid.

My Cup

A minimalist, trimmed body. Clear colors. Kuwata Takuro's "Cup" series began when he was studying at the Tajimi City Pottery Design and Technical Center in Gifu prefecture. The M size is the size most connected to everyday life, the size that Kuwata himself would like to use every day as "My Cup." That is now the basic shape, with S and L sizes added. All three sizes are shown in this

ピカチュウ
Pikachu

[左]各サイズのカップが並ぶ。桑田の提案を受け取った人の数だけ、"使い勝手"という世界が広がる。
[右]エッジが効いた薄いボディ。化粧土のかかる範囲をきっちりと規定するのも桑田独自の工夫。

[left] The various cup sizes, lined up. As people have adopted Kuwata's proposals, the world of user friendliness expands.
[right] The thin body has good edges. Clearly pre-defining the area to apply the colored slip is Kuwata's unique idea.

exhibition.

The distinctive characteristic of this cup series is the use of Gifu's advanced machine mass production technology to create shapes that cannot be made by hand. The balance between the height and diameter and the thickness of each part have been subtly adjusted. At the same time, it has been designed to have a good feel in the hand and at the mouth. The elegantly designed cup may look factory-made at first glance, but each is made, one by one, under the control of the Kuwata studio. They are craft works.

•

More and more

Kuwata's works have clear, bright, and flat coloring. Some of the tones might be called not to be seen in ceramics, but, to Kuwata, that is one experience in what is characteristic of ceramics. "I open the kiln, and gasp! What had been pale blue has turned, after firing at over 1200°C, a striking dark blue. What a delight!" Deeply moved, he has pushed ahead—"More and more," "Over the top."

Those who welcomed those experiments by Kuwata, at an early stage, were people who had not been familiar with ceramic art until then. Their interactive interest, unconstrained by the values of the past but based on liking, encouraged Kuwata and opened up his consciousness to "society." "Encounters drew out new responses from within me. I came to notice things in places I'd never looked at before." This project is one of those delights.

The motif that Kuwata chose for it is a contemporary icon: **Pikachu**. "I felt it had to be Pikachu applied to the cup made while pursuing what could be called the acme, today, of Gifu's mass production technology," a comment filled with his respect. The lean body is formed on a "power machine." He has thoroughly examined the vessel as a contemporary standard, to be comparable to the symbolism that Pikachu have. Then the colorful slip, the thick glaze, the gleam of gold and platinum pigments—the diversity is displayed. Finally, Pikachu, applied using the latest transfer printing technique.

Until the ultimate finishing of the work, the balance of the accidentals and necessities intrinsic to ceramics presents a huge challenge. The richness with which the cups brim with every repetiton of the process is, however, undoubtedly to be received directly, without need of consulting a ceramics dictionary. The knowledge and experience of the Mino ceramics production center, are, however, mobilized in this work and form its backbone. In the cuteness of Pikachu, gushing forth like a fountain from the bottom of the cup, we can trace the enthusiasm of Japanese craftsmanship.

•

Maschine molding: The porcelain clay inserted into the plaster mold is pressed into it while the inner trimmer (a metal rod) is turning, forming the piece between the inner wall of the mold and the spinning trimmer. The thickness of the clay can be changed for each part by adjusting the way the trimmer is applied.

工房｜高くに設けた天井からのトップライトもあり。機能的で快適な環境のデザインが作品の気分に繋がっている。

Studio | Overhead lights in the tall ceiling. The functional, pleasant design of this working environment connects with the mood of his works.

植葉香澄　Ueba Kasumi

光火彩文グラードン｜
Groudon with Flash and Flame Pattern

水文メッソン｜
Sobble with Water Pattern

[上]火炎文ヒバニー茶碗｜
[top] Scorbunny Teabowl with Flame Pattern
[中]唐草文サルノリ茶碗｜
[middle] Grookey Teabowl with Arabesque Pattern
[下]水文メッソン茶碗｜
[bottom] Sobble Teabowl with Water Pattern

羊歯唐草文シェイミ｜
Shaymin with Fern Arabesque Pattern

植葉香澄

Ueba Kasumi

《羊歯唐草文シェイミ茶碗》| 身体を丸めると「はなのように みえるため だれもきづかない」というシェイミ。天地を返すとここでは美味しいドリンクをなみなみと注げる茶碗になる。「かんしゃポケモン」の流儀にならい、優しく包み込み、ありがたく頂戴。
Shaymin Teabowl *with Fern Arabesque Pattern* | When Shaymin curls up, “It is often mistaken for a flowering plant when curled up.” Here, when it is turned upside down it becomes a bowl that can be filled to the brim with delicious beverages. In keeping with the theme of the Gratitude Pokémon, the bowl is to be gently enfolded and drunk from gratefully.

•

もようわくわく

植葉香澄の仕事の印象を決定づけるのは、まずなんといっても圧倒的な文様のパワー。友禅染の絵師だった祖父の影響で、植葉は小さい頃から日本の古典はもちろん、異なるルーツの文様や意匠にも親しんでいました。きっとそれは、知識の集積にとどまらない、感動を伴った体験だったのに違いありません。植葉の文様に対するセンシティブな反応と意欲の迸りが、作品に瑞々しい輝きを与えるのはその証し。文様は付加的な価値ではなく、人の心を動かす力があるという実感が造形の骨格を強固にしています。今回モチーフに選ばれたポケモンたちも、全身余すところなく、色も形もとりどりの文様をまとって晴れやかに登場しました。その思いがけない出会いに驚きながら、目を凝らして隅々まで観察すると、どうもここには読み解きの楽しさもあるみたいです。

　ゲーム『ポケットモンスター ソード・シールド』を遊ぶうえで、プレイヤーは**サルノリ**、**ヒバニー**、**メッソン**という3匹のポケモンのなかから1匹の相棒を選びます。まず、植葉が選んだモチーフはこの3匹。タイトルにもあるとおり、各タイプに合わせてくさ—唐草文、ほのお—火炎文、みず—水文になりました。なるほど納得の設定。しかし分類して安心するだけでなく、さらに想像を逞しくする人もいるのではないでしょうか。たとえばサルノリは、特別なスティックを楽器のように使ってリズミカルな音を鳴らし、植物を成長させるといわれています。一方、唐草文はどこまでも伸びていく蔓の生命力の表象です。なんとも絶妙な組み合わせです。長くたなびく炎。これは走り回ったヒバニーの体をめぐるエネルギーでしょうか。メッソンでは水玉に渦巻、青海波。そこに片輪車という古典的モチーフも見つけたくなるかもしれません。こうしてみると、文様の多くは吉祥のサインであり、そこに人が文様を求める根源的な理由を求められそうです。寿ぎムードが高まったポケモンたちとの日々。ハッピーな光景がますます広がります。

•

Patterns of Delight

The impression made by Ueba Kasumi's works is defined first and foremost by the overwhelming impact of the patterns. Influenced by her grandfather, a *yuzen* dyeing artist, Ueba grew familiar at an early age not only with classical Japanese patterns, but

グラードン
Groudon

シェイミ（ランドフォルム）
Shaymin
Land Forme

サルノリ
Grookey

ヒバニー
Scorbunny

メッソン
Sobble

[左]《光火彩文グラードン》(制作中・部分) | 迫力のボディに花を生けられる。見逃せないチャームポイント。
[中]《水文メッソン》(制作中) | 美しい文様には美しいボディ。オブジェクトとして自立するギリギリの頭身バランスに迫った。花器で(も)ある。矢印部分をご覧あれ。いける植物の種類、長さ。メッソン花器に似合った場と置く角度。調度としての可能性を思い描く喜びが、小さな開口部から広がる。
[右]《唐草文サルノリ茶碗》(制作中) | 文様のにぎわいの下に土の柔らかなボディ。首をかしげてこちらを見る姿が愛らしい。確かな造形はモチーフのインパクトとはうらはらに、意外なほどに手に馴染むプロポーションとなっている。目と手で交流を結ぶ、ティータイムのよき仲間を発見。

[left] *Groudon with Flame Pattern* (in progress, detail) | Flowers can be arranged in its powerful body—a charming point not to be missed.
[middle] *Sobble with Water Pattern* (in progress)| A beautiful body for a beautiful pattern. The balance of head and body is calculated so it just manages to stand on its own as an object. It is (also) a vase. Look at the part where the arrow is pointing: through this small opening expand the joys of envisioning the Sobble vase's possibilities, the types and lengths of the plants that can be arranged, where it should be placed and at what angle.
[right] *Grookey Teabowl with Arabesque Pattern* (in progress) | This is the soft clay body beneath the lively patterns. The figure tilting its head to look at us is charming. The solidly designed object, belying the impact of the motif, has proportions that are surprisingly comfortable in the hand. A fine companion for teatime, with whom to interact through hand and eye.

also with designs and patterns with roots overseas. This must have been a profound experience that transcended mere accumulation of knowledge, as demonstrated by Ueba's sensitive response to patterns and the outpouring of ambition that gives her work its freshness and luster. The strength of Ueba's modeling is heightened by her realization that patterns are more than added-on value, and have the power to move people's hearts and minds. The Pokémon she chose as motifs for this exhibition are all bedecked with patterns in a variety of colors and shapes, and appear as radiant presences. Surprised by this unexpected encounter, one looks closely and observes every inch of the works, and it is evident that there is a lot of interpreting and deciphering to be done here.

In the video games *Pokémon Sword and Pokémon Shield*, the player chooses a partner from among three Pokémon: **Grookey**, **Scorbunny**, and **Sobble**. Ueba chose these three as her subjects. As the title suggests, the patterns were chosen to match each Pokémon type: Grass –arabesques, Fire –a flame pattern, and Water –a ripple pattern. This all makes sense. However, beyond placing things in neat, reassuring categories, they may also stimulate the imaginations of some viewers. For example: it is said that Grookey uses its special stick like a musical tool to beat a rhythmic sound, which then causes the plants to grow. On the other hand, the arabesque pattern is a representation of the life force of a vine that extends forever. It seems to be an exquisite combination. The long, fluttering flames may represent Scorbunny's physical energy as it runs around. Meanwhile, Sobble is represented by polka dots, swirls, and blue waves. One might be reminded of the classical motif of the *katawaguruma* (single cartwheel). In this way, many of the patterns are auspicious signs, and here, it seems to find the fundamental meaning why people seek patterns. Along with images of jubilant life with Pokémon, joyful scenes expand ever outward.

桝本佳子　Masumoto Keiko

リザードン／信楽壷 | Charizard / Shigaraki Jar

信楽壷／ファイヤー｜Shigaraki Jar / Moltres

[左] ロコン／信楽壷 | [left] Vulpix / Shigaraki Jar
[右] 信楽壷／キュウコン | [right] Shigaraki Jar / Ninetales

[上]キャモメ／染付皿｜[top] Wingull / Underglazed Plate
[中]タマンタ／染付皿｜[middle] Mantyke / Underglazed Plate
[下]ポッチャマ／染付皿｜[bottom] Piplup / Underglazed Plate

陶磁
Ceramics

桝本佳子

Masumoto Keiko

器×装飾

「器と装飾の、主と従という関係を壊すこと」。これは桝本佳子が長年追いかけているテーマです。小学生のときに茶道の稽古に行ったのがきっかけで、陶芸に興味を持った桝本は、大学で陶芸を専攻。が、校内の風潮はどうも「器をやるよりも考えることがあるらしい」く、入学早々に戸惑いました。器要素の完全排除もやってはみたものの、馴染むどころか、そういう志向が自分のなかにないことに気づくばかり。戦後日本の工芸界でさかんになったいわゆる“オブジェ”の制作では、機能を封印した跡地に作者の内面や素材との対話を詩情豊かに映す傾向がありました。しかし桝本にはそれがなんとも気恥ずかしく、「もっとカラッとできないか。(内省的な)ジメジメ感とは距離を取りたかった」。そこで行き着いたのが現在のスタイルです。

今回も器からポケモンが飛び出し、あるいはポケモンが器を切り取った、エネルギッシュでユーモアに満ちた作品が登場しました。両者がっぷり四つに組み、時に浸食し合い、時に意外な方向から協働する様子を見ていると、かえってポケモンと工芸それぞれの原像に近づける気もします。

ほのおタイプ、みずタイプ

本展の企画趣旨を伝えたとき、即座に「ほのおタイプ」と決めた桝本。「単純だけれど炎は焼きものと切り離せない」。そこから穴窯での焼成の検討が始まりました。桝本の婚家は滋賀県信楽のみはる窯。鎌倉時代から続く信楽焼のパワーが、ポケモンの「ほのお」の相を顕わにしました。実は桝本にとって、信楽焼での本格

❶窯出し | 穴窯で4日間、昼夜薪をくべて焼成。その後1週間待つ。経験豊富な家族と歴史ある窯業地ならではのサポートが制作の大きな力となった。《リザードン》は窯に入るギリギリのサイズ。
❷《リザードン》の炎パーツ。本体ともども家族の作品と一緒に焼成。
❸本焼後の《ファイヤー》。これから上絵付で花文を描き、春の気配をまとわせる。

❶ Removal from kiln after firing | The piece was fired in an *anagama* for four days with wood burning day and night, and then left to sit for one week. The support of experienced family members and the historic kiln site were of great help in the production process. The figure of *Charizard* is so large it barely fit in the kiln.
❷ The flame parts of *Charizard*. Like the main body, they were fired along with the family's pottery.
❸ *Moltres* after second firing. After this a floral design was painted in overglaze enamel to give the work a hint of spring.

リザードン
Charizard

ロコン
Vulpix

キュウコン
Ninetales

ファイヤー
Moltres

的な制作は今回が初挑戦なのだとか。「今までの自分には信楽焼で表すべきモチーフがなかったけれど、今回はバチーッときた」。窯詰め、薪の投げ入れ方1つで表情も形状も変わり、そのうえ偶発性も免れないなか、火のコントロールが成功した《**ロコン**》は、緋色と白の抜けのバランスが上手くいったと大満足。超重量級の《**リザードン**》は予想の3倍くらい変形しましたが、「それも穴窯らしい」迫力へと繋がりました。

さて、焼締の強さを“信楽”タイプの特色とするならば、“染付”では潤むような艶と質感を目と手で味わいたくなります。「もともと焼きものらしくて好き」だった染付の皿には、「みず」タイプのポケモンたちが招かれました。皿は卓上に平置きするのはもちろん、壁に掛けても良さが生きるのは世界各地の調度として実証済み。そこで選んだポケモンたちのうち、3種は「ひこう」タイプも兼ね備えています。青の美しさに海を想うか天を仰ぐかは鑑賞者次第。あしらわれた模様がどちら由来なのか、謎解きの楽しさも用意されています。

•

Vessels × Decoration

“To disrupt the master-servant relationship between vessels and their decoration”: This is a theme that Masumoto Keiko has been pursuing for many years. Masumoto became interested in ceramics after attending tea ceremony lessons during elementary school, and majored in ceramics while at university. However, upon entering university she was perplexed because the ethos of the school seemed to be that “there are more important things to think about than making vessels.” She attempted to completely eliminate the vessel element, but instead of getting used to its absence, she only became more aware that this was not her true calling. In the production of “art objects,” which gained popularity in the world of postwar Japanese craft, there was a tendency to poetically represent the artist’s inner self and dialogue with the material in forms devoid of functionality. Masumoto, however, felt somewhat awkward about this, and wondered, “Why can’t I be frank and open? I wanted to distance myself from a gloomy feeling (of introspection).” That was how she arrived at her current style.

In the energetic and humorous works in the current exhibit, Pokémon appear to jump from the vessels, or cut out the forms of vessels. Watching the Pokémon and vessels firmly interlocking, sometimes eroding each other, sometimes moving together in unexpected directions, we may feel as though she was actually drawing closer to the original images of both Pokémon and craft.

•

Fire Type and Water Type

When Masumoto was told about the concept of this exhibition, she immediately decided on Fire-type Pokémon. According to Masumoto, “It’s a simplistic reason, but that’s because fire is inseparable from pottery.” She then began exploring the option of firing in an *anagama*, a type of kiln that goes back to ancient times. Masumoto married into a family located in Shigaraki, Shiga Prefecture which runs the Miharu Kiln. The power of Shigaraki ware, which has been made since the Kamakura Period (circa. late 12th century to 1333), fully embodies the nature of Fire-type Pokémon. This was the first time Masumoto had attempted full-scale production of Shigaraki ware. She says, “Until now I had no motif I wanted to express with Shigaraki ware, but this time, it just clicked.” The look and form of the ceramics can easily change depending on how it is inserted in the kiln and how the firewood is thrown in. And while unexpected occurrences are unavoidable, she was very satisfied with the **Vulpix** jar, for which the kiln’s fire was successfully controlled and a balance between scarlet and white was achieved. The super-heavyweight **Charizard** was about three times as deformed as expected, but this was connected to the power of the *anagama* and “shows the unique charm of this type of kiln.”

If the strength of *yakishime* (unglazed ware fired at high temperatures) is considered to be a characteristic of Shigaraki ware, *sometsuke* (unglazed ware painted with cobalt pigment) attracts us for its visual and tacticle experience of the moist luster and texture. Water-type Pokémon were summoned to appear on *sometsuke* plates, which she had always liked because “they look like typical pottery.” Plates have a proven track record around the world, not only as dishes to be laid flat on a tabletop, but also as decorations hung on a wall to showcase their beauty. She also selected three Flying-type Pokémon. Whether the beautiful blue represents the sea or the heavens is up to the viewer’s judgment. The viewer can also enjoy pondering the riddle of where (sea or sky) the decorative patterns originated.

《キュウコン》(部分)|キュウコンは「9人の聖者が合体しキュウコンになったという伝説も残る」ポケモン。その伝説から着想を得て、九賢人のいる光景を染付で表現。穴窯で焼くと染付が流れやすいが「それも古い感じが出て面白い」。

Ninetales (detail) | Ninetales is a Pokémon believed to have come into existence when nine wizards possessing sacred powers merged into one. Inspired by this legend, Masumoto represented the scene of the nine sages in underglaze blue. Underglaze blue tends to run when fired in an *anagama* kiln, she says, “This effect intrigues me because it gives the piece an old-fashioned feel.”

キャモメ
Wingull

ポッチャマ
Piplup

タマンタ
Mantyke

水橋さおり Mizuhashi Saori

友禅帯「閃光」| Sash, "Flash," *Yuzen* Dyeing

友禅訪問着「群」｜
Kimono, “Herd,”
Yuzen Dyeing

水橋さおり
Mizuhashi Saori

きものよきもの

水橋さおりの着物好きは祖母譲り。子どもの頃は織とか染めとかの区別はなく、美しいもの、良いものといえば着物であり、長じて「日本の手仕事」が気になり出してからも、行き着くところはやはり着物に関わることでした。

工芸実習のある短大で座学のみだった友禅が妙にカッコよく思われて、卒業後、あらためて着物の総合教育を謳う専門学校に進学。そこで初めての「友禅」に挑戦しました。友禅染のいくつもある工程のなかで、特に模様部分に色を挿すことを友禅といいますが、筆に含ませた染料が絹地に染み込んでいくその瞬間、「こんなにも綺麗なものがあるのか」と水橋の心は震えたのだそうです。

短大で実習した型染や蠟染も、手段は違えども同じ毛細管現象を原理とする染めであることに変わりなかったはずです。しかし技法を部分的に取り出して体験するのと、目の前の行為の先に衣裳制作を置くのとでは現象を把捉する精度が異なったのかもしれません。「輝いて見えた」この瞬間の記憶が、今なお水橋を制作に向かわせる引力となっているようです。

距離

水橋に全工程のなかで一番好きな工程を尋ねると、迷わず「糸目糊」と答えました。遠目には花尽しかとも思えた《友禅訪問着「群」》ですが、近づけば**メリープ**と**モココ**が大集合。これら1匹1匹の、やわらかな輪郭からとりどりの表情、渦巻く毛並みまで表したごく細の白線が糸目糊の跡です。袋に圧をかけて糊を絞る。線を引く。2つの動作を同時に行う様子は意外にもスピーディです。確かにそうでなくては線がだれ、モチーフの生命感も減じてしまうに違いありません。

《友禅帯「閃光」》には、お太鼓結びを想定した位置に**メガデンリュウ**が登場。地色は後退色の濃藍で奥行感を、対してメガデンリュウのボディに挿した暖かな黄色は進出感を増幅させました。どことなく宇宙めいた雰囲気なのは、メガデンリュウ（デンリュウ）のしっぽの先の輝きがはるか遠く、宇宙まで届くという設定に思いをめぐらせたから。物語性を意匠に取り入れるのも友禅ならではの妙味です。

友禅：江戸時代に始まった糊置防染法による模様染の1つ。名称は元禄期に評判をとった扇絵師・宮崎友禅斎に由来。糸目糊と呼ばれる細い防染糊で描く輪郭線は、近接する色のにじみを防いで多彩な色彩を可能とし、また細密描写の道も開いた。下絵・糊置・色挿・伏糊・地染など高度な技術による多数の工程を経て完成する。

Kimono Delight

Mizuhashi Saori's love of the kimono is inherited from her grandmother. As a child, she didn't distinguish between weaving and dyeing but just knew that the kimono meant something beautiful, something good. As an extension of that experience, she became interested in Japanese handicrafts and, not surprisingly, where that took her was related to the kimono.

At a junior college that offered training in crafts, she thought that *yuzen* textiles, which were only discussed in the classroom, with no hands-on training, were remarkably attractive. After graduation, she studied at a technical school that provided comprehensive education about the kimono. There she tackled her first *yuzen* project. Among the processes involved in its creation, adding color to a pattern is called "*yuzen*." At the moment of the pigment with which the brush is filled permeates the silk ground, Mizuhashi's heart was stirred. "Could there really be something this lovely?"

In theory, the technique should not have differed from the stencil- and wax-dyeing methods she practiced at junior college, as they all relied on capillary action. However, the accuracy of grasping the phenomenon may have differed between partially extracting the technique for experience and practicing the technique with having making costumes as the goal. "It appeared, glowing": Her memory of that moment is the attraction that directs Mizuhashi to creating, even now.

Distance

When we asked Mizuhashi what part of the process she liked best, she said, without hesitation, "Applying the lines of paste." Her *Kimono, "Herd," Yuzen dyeing*, has a pattern that appears, seen from a distance, to filled with flowers, but a closer look reveals great gatherings of images of **Mareep** and **Flaaffy**. The extremely fine white lines that express the soft contours of each Pokémon,

メリープ
Mareep

モココ
Flaaffy

デンリュウ
Ampharos

メガデンリュウ
Mega Ampharos

their various expressions, and their swirling fleece all resulted as traces from lines of paste Mizuhashi applied. That involves two actions: applying pressure on the tube that holds the glue and then drawing the line. Those two actions, performed simultaneously, are extraordinarily speedy. Indeed, if not done swiftly, the line would weaken and the motif would lose its liveliness.

In the *Sash, "Flash," Yuzen dyeing*, Mizuhashi has planned the design, on the assumption that the *obi* will be tied in a *taiko-musubi* knot, so that **Mega Ampharos** is positioned to appear. The base color is dark indigo blue, a receding color, which gives a sense of depth. The warm yellow of Mega Ampharos's body, by contrast, amplifies a sense of movement. The somewhat cosmic appearance is obtained by extending the glow at the end of Mega Ampharos's tail so that it appears to extend far into space. This incorporation of a narrative quality in the design is one of the charms of *yuzen*.

•

Yuzen: One of the patterns dyeing by the past resist method that started in the Edo period. The name comes from Miyazaki Yuzensai, a fan painter who was popular during the Genroku period. The contour lines drawn with a thin anti-dyeing paste called *itome-nori* prevented adjacent colors from bleeding and enabled a variety of colors, and also opened the way for detailed depiction. It is completed through a number of processes using advanced techniques such as sketching, pasting, color insertion, glue paste, and ground dyeing.

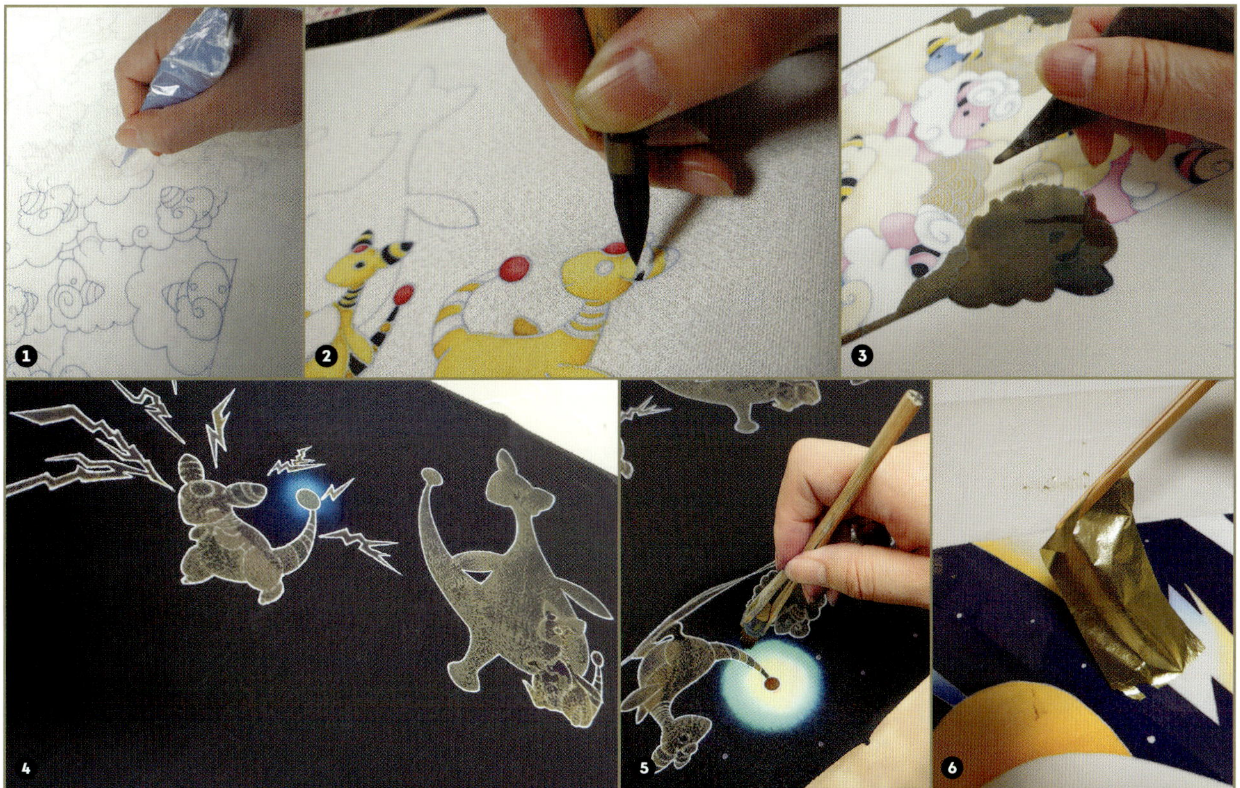

❶糸目糊｜モココの毛並みのどこかに「でんきショック」「メリープをかわいがってあげてね」などの隠し文字も。洒落を楽しむ趣向もまた友禅の伝統。
❷色挿｜《閃光》(前柄部分)
❸伏糊[ふせのり]｜色挿しした模様部分を糊で覆い、刷毛で地色を一気に染める引染に備える。
❹糸目糊→色挿→伏糊→引染を終えた《閃光》(前柄部分)。このあとに「蒸し」(染料を生地にしっかり定着させる)と水元[みずもと](糊や余分な染料を洗い流す)などの工程が続く。
❺繊細な暈しでデンリュウのしっぽの先に灯る光を表現。
❻箔置｜専用の糊を生地に置き、金箔を押して、メガデンリュウが放つ光のパワーを拡張。

❶ Lines of paste | Words are hidden in Flaaffy's wool: "Thunder Shock" and "Take good care of Flaaffy," for example. Enjoying jokes and puns is also part of the *yuzen* tradition.
❷ Applying the dye (*Flash*, front part of the pattern)
❸ Covering with paste | The parts of the pattern to which dye has been applied are covered with glue, and a brush is used to dye the background color all at once.
❹ Applying the line of paste → applying dye → covering with paste → brush application of dye, all completed *Flash* (front pattern of the sash). Subsequent steps include steaming, to help the dye bond with the fabric, and rinsing, to remove the glue and excess dye.
❺ Delicate shading makes the light glow on the tip of Ampharos's tail.
❻ Applying gold leaf | A special glue is placed on the fabric and gold leaf pressed on it, amplifying the power of the light that Mega Ampharos emits.

小宮康義　Komiya Yasuyoshi

江戸小紋 着尺「タマゲタケ・モロバレル」｜
Kimono Cloth, Edo *Komon*, “Foongus and Amoonguss”

江戸小紋 着尺「フライゴン」|
Kimono Cloth, Edo *Komon*, "Flygon"

江戸小紋 着尺「ガラルマッギョ」｜
Kimono Cloth, Edo *Komon*, "Galarian Stunfisk"

江戸小紋 着尺「ゲンガー・ゴースト」|
Kimono Cloth, Edo *Komon*, “Gengar and Haunter”

小宮康義

Komiya Yasuyoshi

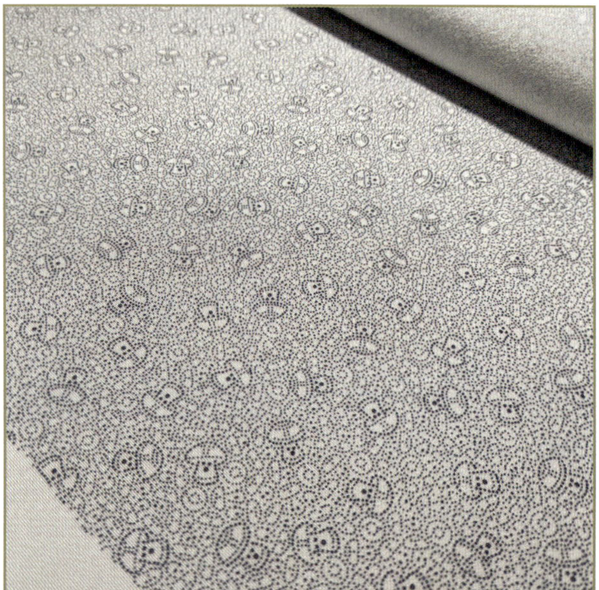

[上]型付《タマゲタケ・モロバレル》｜糊に入れた群青(合成顔料)は染めたあと酸で洗うと分解され、白く抜けた文様となる。
[下]《フライゴン》型紙　彫：今坂千秋
[top] Stencil printing: *Foongus and Amoonguss.* | The fabric, with the paste resist in place, has been dyed with a dark blue pigment (a synthetic dye). It will then be washed in an acid solution to dissolve the paste so that the white motifs rise up against the background color.
[bottom] Stencil for *Flygon* (carver: Imasaka Chiaki)

油断大敵

江戸小紋は型染の1種で、構成要素は点・線・面。ものすごくミニマムで、遠く色無地と見たものが、近づけば驚きの充実の模様世界が広がります。そんな江戸小紋のもくろみと「同じじゃないか。これは小紋でやるべきだ」と小宮康義が選んだのは《タマゲタケ・モロバレル》と《ガラルマッギョ》。

　モンスターボールによく似たカサをもつ**タマゲタケ**は、猛毒の胞子を吹き出します。作品中でも両者は判別しがたいので要注意。一方、**モロバレル**は点も気持ち大きくされたのでモロにバレ、ふわりと舞い上がる感じも楽しい。《ガラルマッギョ》は、今回、小宮がゲーム内で出会ったポケモンです。土に半ば埋まったモンスターボール。かと思えば実は**マッギョ(ガラルのすがた)**のくちびるで、飛び出し、トゲトゲした歯で食いついて離さないのだとか。3つ山の形はマッギョの模様か、それとも葉っぱ、あるいは誰かの足跡？ トラップポケモンの生息地を歩き回るなんて恐ろしい…とつぶやくそばから洒落た設定にニヤニヤ止まらず、目はますます釘づけとなります。

文様の気分

ポケモンたちの形姿をパズルみたいに組んだ《**フライゴン**》と《**ゲンガー・ゴースト**》。ポケモンの生態と、それぞれの文様の造形が放つ気分と重なりました。砂嵐も起こすフライゴンの羽部分は、江戸小紋と呼ぶギリギリのサイズ感。孔を開けた型紙の物理的にもギリギリの配分でしたが、おかげで染め抜かれた白が連続し、生地いっぱいに吹きわたる清爽の風を呼び起こしました。立涌は対向する曲線2本単位で構成し、水蒸気が涌き立ちのぼるさまに見立てられる伝統文様です。ここでは斜めに振られ、ガスじょうポケモンのゴーストの浮遊感とピッタリはまりました。しなやかな絹の艶とドレープに寄り添う陰影に、神出鬼没なゴーストを追うスリルが増しそうです。

　ところで隠れ上手なゲンガーを見つけられたでしょうか。ヒントは「己が影 ひとりでに 笑いしとき」…？ 皆さんの目と向き合うタイミングをヒッソリ窺っているようです。

ゴースト
Haunter

ゲンガー
Gengar

フライゴン
Flygon

タマゲタケ
Foongus

モロバレル
Amoonguss

マッギョ
ガラルのすがた
Galarian Stunfisk

江戸小紋：江戸時代、諸大名が着用した裃(かみしも)の模様付が発祥とされる白抜きの型染で、基本的に絹地に単色染め。文様は極めて細かく、刃先が半円形の彫刻刀を型紙に立て、くるりと回転させて彫り出す錐彫(きりぼり)の点が3cm四方に900個以上染め抜かれるものもある。今回の型紙には錐彫と文様の形に作られた突き道具で彫る道具彫を併用。板に生地を張り、型紙を置いて糊防染したあと、地色を引き染めする。近代以降は合成染料を糊に入れた色糊を塗布して地染するシゴキ技法が使われるようになった。

江戸小紋という名称は、小宮康義の曾祖父・小宮康助の1955年の重要無形文化財保持者（人間国宝）認定に際し、その他の小紋と区別するために考案された。

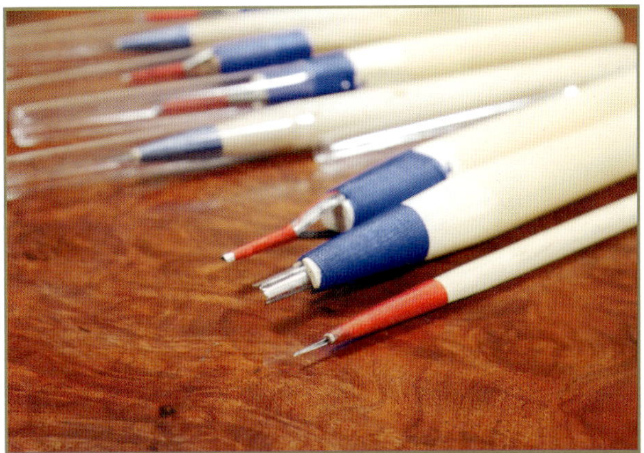

型紙用の刃物｜型紙を彫る人が自作することが多い。
Carving knives for making stencils | Many stencil carvers make their own carving knives.

Don't Let Your Guard Down

Edo *komon* is a type of fine stencil dyeing, in which the elements of composition are point, line, and plane. The designs are extraordinarily small, so that, viewed from a distance, the fabric appears to be plain colored cloth. Come closer, however, a world of motifs, amazingly fully developed, unfolds. Saying of the Pokémon designs and Edo *komon*, "They're just alike. I should make *komon* of them," Komiya Yasuyoshi chose Foongus, Amoonguss, and Galarian Stunfisk.

Foongus has a mushroom cap that resembles a Poké Ball. When someone carelessly gets close to it, it squirts out ferociously poisonous spores. In creating the Edo *komon*, it was hard to distinguish the renderings of a Poké Ball and Foongus. Caution is needed! For **Amoonguss**, however, he drew the dots slightly larger, making it easier to find the characters in the pattern. It's fun to see Amoonguss float softly in the design. **Galarian Stunfisk** is a Pokémon that Komiya met in a game. It appears as a Poké Ball, half buried in the ground. But wait—it has a beak, and once it leaps out and sinks its jagged teeth into something, it won't let go. The shape of the three hills might be a Stunfisk motif or leaves or maybe someone's footprint! Though it would be scary to wander around the Trap Pokémon's habitat, it's hard not to grin at the witty setup, with eyes glued on the Galarian Stunfisk.

The Moods of the Motifs

The Pokémon forms in each of the designs are combined like puzzles. Here we have the *Flygon* and *Gengar and Haunter* designs. The Pokémon ecology overlaps with the mood that the forms of each of the motifs generate. The wings of the **Flygon**, which can stir up sandstorms, seem to be of a size that just barely fits the Edo *Komon* definition. The stencil paper for the Flygon also just barely managed to accommodate the design's being arranged physically on it, in order to open the holes for the pattern. The result is that the white areas, left undyed, link together and call up a fresh breeze that blows all across the fabric. The *tatewaku* pattern, a traditional motif, is composed of two wavy lines on opposite sides, creating an effect that is likened to steam rising. Those patterns, applied on the diagonal, are a perfect match for the floating effect of the Gas Pokémon, **Haunter**. The luster of the glossy silk and the shadows that the draping creates add to the thrill of chasing the elusive ghost.

But **Gengar** is an expert at concealment—have you found it? The hint is "If your shadow starts to laugh"—Gengar may be lurking there. It's secretly peeping to see when viewers' eyes turn its way.

Edo *komon*: Edo Komon is basically a technique for dyeing in a single color on silk, using stencil dyeing to reserve the white of the silk ground. It originated in the Edo period as the technique for dyeing the fine motifs on the ceremonial *kamishimo* (vest and loose, pleated over-trouser) that *daimyo* wore. The motifs are extremely fine. By applying a carving knife with a semicircular tip vertically to the stencil paper and rotating the blade, the stencil carver drill holes in it (*kiribori*). With this tool, 900 or more holes (to which paste resist will be applied) may be carved inside a square three centimeters on a side. Carving knives for *kiribori* and *dogubori* ("tool punching") were used to create the stencils for this project. In *dogubori*, the tip of the knife used is prepared in the shape of the motif to be carved, the knife is applied vertically, and the pattern is punched out of the stencil paper. After the stencil is applied to the undyed cloth, which is stretched on a board, and the resist paste applied, the dye for the background color is brushed on. In modern times, the *shigoki* method has come to be used. Instead of brushing on the dye, an artificial dye is mixed with a soft paste, and that colored paste applied to the fabric, with a spatula, to dye it.

The name Edo *komon* was given to that technique in 1955, to distinguish it from other *komon* dyeing techniques, when Komiya Yasuyoshi's great-grandfather, Komiya Kosuke, was designated a holder of an Important Intangible Cultural Property (Living National Treasure) for Edo *komon*.

ポケモン×工芸
美とわざの大発見

POKÉMON×KOGEI
Playful Encounters of Pokémon and Japanese Craft

●

作家略歴・参考文献

編：横川悠子、日南日和［国立工芸館］

Artists Biography

Edit: Yokogawa Yuko, Himinami Hiyori
[National Crafts Museum]

●

作品リスト
List of Works

池田晃将 | Ikeda Terumasa

1987 千葉県生まれ
2016 金沢美術工芸大学大学院修士課程修了
2019 金沢卯辰山工芸工房修了
2020 独立、金沢市内に工房を構える

1987 Born in Chiba Prefecture
2016 Completes master's program at Kanazawa College of Art
2019 Completes training program at Kanazawa Utatsuyama Kogei Kobo (Crafts Workshop)
2020 Opens own workshop in Kanazawa

主な個展

2014 「池田晃将 漆展―極小の装飾―」(Café&gallery Musee/石川)
2015 「池田晃将―漆加飾の小細工展―」(伊勢丹新宿本店5階ウエストパーク/東京)
2019 「電光装飾―Cyber Effect―池田晃将漆芸展」(日本橋高島屋6階美術工芸サロン/東京)
2020 「池田晃将漆芸展」(しぶや黒田陶苑/東京)
2021 「池田晃将の螺鈿」(銀座一穂堂/東京)
「池田晃将展」(新風館/京都)
2022 「池田晃将展」(日本橋高島屋6階美術工芸サロン/東京)
2023 「Terumasa Ikeda: Iridescent Lacquer」(Ippodo gallery/ニューヨーク)

主なグループ展

2014 「次世代工芸展」(京都市美術館別館)
「Epoch Garden」(金沢市問屋町スタジオ/石川)
2015 「コウゲイ℃―素材と今の接触点―」(金沢21世紀美術館市民ギャラリーB/石川)
2016 「漆芸の未来を拓く―生新の時2016―」(輪島漆芸美術館/石川)
2017 「Singapore Contemporary Art Show」(Suntec Exhibition Centre SINGAPORE/シンガポール)
「結晶する漆―Essence of URUSHI―」(日本橋三越本店/東京)
2018 「第3回翔ぶ鳥展」(銀座一穂堂/東京)['19, '20]
「なつめ」(しぶや黒田陶苑/東京)
「Art Expo New York」(Pier94 U.S.A./ニューヨーク)
「もう一つの工芸未来派」(和光ホール/東京)
2020 「和巧絶佳展―令和時代の超工芸―」(パナソニック汐留美術館/東京)
2021 高島屋創業190周年「悉皆(shikkai)―風の時代の継承者たち―」(日本橋高島屋/東京ほか4会場)
「《十二の鷹》と明治の工芸―万博出品時代から今日まで 変わりゆく姿」(国立工芸館/石川)
「現代漆のチカラ展」(福屋八丁堀本展7階美術画廊/広島)
2022 「工芸の表現四人展」(和光ホール/東京)
「ジャンルレス工芸展」(国立工芸館/石川)

展覧会図録

- 『金沢工芸アート・チャリティーオークション』、金沢21世紀美術館・金沢アートグミ、2015年
- 『漆芸の未来を拓く 生新の時』、輪島漆芸美術館、2016
- 『なつめ 特別展』、しぶや黒田陶苑、2018年
- 『第3回 翔ぶ鳥展』、銀座一穂堂、2018年[第4回:2019年、第5回:2020年]
- 『池田晃将漆芸展:電光装飾―Cyber effect―』、日本橋高島屋本館6階美術工芸サロン、2019年
- 『和巧絶佳 令和時代の超工芸』、パナソニック汐留美術館、2020年
- 『現代漆のチカラ展』、福屋八丁堀店、2021年
- 『池田晃将の螺鈿』、Ippodo Gallery、2021年
- 『悉皆 風の時代の継承者たち 高島屋創業190周年』、高島屋日本橋店本館6階美術画廊ほか、2021年
- 『池田晃将展』、新風館、2021年
- 『《十二の鷹》と明治の工芸 万博出品時代から今日まで 変わりゆく姿』、国立工芸館、2021年
- 『ジャンルレス工芸』、国立工芸館、2022年

書籍

- 『工芸の国、ニッポン 一〇〇年残るもの、一〇〇年受け継ぐもの』(別冊太陽)、平凡社、2020年
- 橋本麻里『かざる日本』、岩波書店、2021年

定期刊行物

- 「若き超絶技巧の作り手たち」『婦人画報』No.1416、ハースト婦人画報社、2021年7月号
- 「ナニコレ!?スゴ技アート」『月刊北國アクタス』No.393、北國新聞社、2022年4月号

WEB

- 『Terumasa-ikeda.com: 池田晃将オフィシャルサイト』(https://www.terumasa-ikeda.com/)[2022年12月27日最終アクセス]
- 『池田晃将 公式特設サイト』(https://terumasa-ikeda.jp/)[2022年12月27日最終アクセス]

池本一三 | Ikemoto Kazumi

1954 京都府生まれ
1978 京都市立芸術大学美術学部西洋画学科卒業
1997 多摩美術大学美術学部工芸学科助教授、教授(2007-2023)
現在、名誉教授(2024-)

1954 Born in Kyoto
1978 Graduates from the Faculty of Fine Arts, Kyoto City University of Arts, majoring in western painting
1997 Becomes Associate Assistant Professor in the Department of Ceramic, Glass, and Metal Works, Faculty of Art and Design, Tama Art University (Professor Emeritus since 2024)

主な個展
1988 個展(池袋西武百貨店/東京)
1991 個展(渋谷西武百貨店/東京)
1993 個展(ギャラリーα/東京)
1994 個展(GALERIE L/ハンブルグ)
1995 個展(COMPOSITION GALLEREY/サンフランシスコ)
1997 個展(コンテンポラリーアートNIKI/東京)
2004 個展(心斎橋大丸/大阪)
2005 個展(ギャラリーやぶき/岡山)
2007 個展(chappele gallery/ニューヨーク)

主なグループ展
1977 「独立美術展」(東京都美術館)
「3人展」(菊池画廊/京都)
1978 「GLASS Exhibition」(倉敷IVY-SQUARE/岡山)
「現代日本のガラス展」(D.Erlien Fine Arts/ミルウォーキー)['87]
1979 「ステンドクラスandモザイク展」(岡山天満屋)
1980 「ステンドクラス4人展」(日本イタリア京都会館)
1982 「グラス7人展」(京都新聞社ギャラリー)
1987 「'87 日本のガラス展」(新宿小田急百貨店11Fグランドギャラリー/東京・天神岩田屋本館8F催場/福岡)
1987 「NEW GLASS REVIEW 8」(Corning Museum of Glass/ニューヨーク)['92, '02, '07]
1988 「第3回世界現代ガラス展」(北海道立近代美術館)['91, '94]
1989 「現代工芸の一断面展」(麻布美術工芸館/東京)
「第8回国際ガラス展」(HABATAT GALERIES/フロリダ)[第21回:'93/ミシガン, 第22回:'94/ミシガン]
1990 「90' 現代ガラスの造形展」(箱根彫刻の森美術館/神奈川)
「東京ガラスアート展」(有楽町阪急8階コミュニティギャラリー/東京)
1993 「NEW GLASS in JAPAN」(KUNST MUSEUM/ドイツ)
1995 「BARE ESSETIALS展」(SINGNATURE/ボストン、マシュピーチェストナツヒル)
「GLASS in AUSTRALIA」(ミートマーケットクラフトセンター/メルボルン)
1996 「Winds from the East and North」(The Nordic House Reykjavik/アイスランド)
1997 「Made in japan Exhibition」(GLAS MUSEUM/デンマーク)
1998 「いまを表現するガラス造形展」(新潟市美術館)
1999 「日本のガラス2000年 弥生から現代まで」(サントリー美術館/東京)
2000 「Contemporary Japanese Glass Art Exhibition」(The Grand Crystal Museum Taipei/台湾)
2001 「ガラスの魅力展 21世紀を造形するアーティストたち 日本ガラス教育の一断面 スタジオ・グラス運動の受容と富山市のとりくみ」(姫路市立美術館/兵庫)
「二人展」(東急百貨店渋谷本店/東京)
「ガラスに描く、光と彩りの2000年」(サントリー美術館/東京)
2003 「二人展」(伊勢丹府中店/東京)
「OUT SPOKEN GLASS展」(北海道立近代美術館)
2004 「二人展」(chappele gallery/ジョージア)['05]
「第32回国際ガラス展」(HABATAT GALLERIES/ミシガン)
2006 「植物のかたち6人展」(ルーフギャラリー、髙島屋玉川店/東京)
「日本の現代ガラス展」(Plateaux Gallery/ロンドン)
2008 「Frozen Music: Glass in the Garden」(Portland Japanese Garden/ポートランド)
2009 「ガラスマスターズ展」(東急百貨店渋谷本店/東京)
「Fun to Vessel 2人展」(東急百貨店渋谷本店/東京)
「3 Nations Asian Contemporary Glass Art」(Gallerey Sklo/ソウル・Koru Contemporary Art/香港)
2011 「Voice of glass」(ラトビア美術大学)
「10x10 exhibition」(Pittsburgh GlPittsburgh Glass Center/ペンシルベニア)
2012 「池本一三、小田橋昌代 2人展」(瀬戸市新世紀工芸館/愛知)
「Glass Masters of Japan and the North American Studio Glass Movement」(Willard Wankelman Gallery/アメリカ)
「Japanese Art and Design」(Museum of Arts and Design/ニューヨーク)
2013 「2人展」(JR名古屋髙島屋/名古屋)['15]
2014 「2人展」(髙島屋ギャラリーNext/大阪)['16, '19]
「ガラス工芸展」(なかとみ現代工芸館/山梨)
「コンテンポラリーグラス展」(東急百貨店渋谷本店/東京)
2015 「2人展」(京都髙島屋)
「タマビガラス展」(多摩美術大学美術館/東京)
「あづみ野ガラス工房30周年記念展」(安曇野市豊科近代美術館/長野)
2017 「2人展」(池袋西武百貨店/東京)['19, '22]
「2人展」(乾ギャラリー/茨城)['19]

主な受賞歴

1987 「'87日本のガラス展」奨励賞
1990 「東京ガラスアート展」佳作
2004 「第32回国際ガラス展」審査員賞

展覧会図録

- 『世界現代ガラス展』、北海道立近代美術館ほか、1982年
- 『地水火風 コスミック・イメージの饗宴 現代工芸の一断面』、工芸学会麻布美術工芸館、1989年
- 『'90 現代ガラスの造形展』、彫刻の森美術館、1990年
- 『ガラスに描く、光と彩りの2000年 古代エジプトからグラス・アートまで』、サントリー美術館、2002年
- 『The 32nd Annual International Glass Invitational: the Awards Exhibition』、Habarar Galleries Michigan、2004年
- 『ガラス工芸の精華 ガレから現代まで』、瀬戸市美術館ほか、2009年
- 『タマビガラス キラキラ・ワクワク・ドキドキ』、多摩美術大学美術館、2015年

書籍

- 『ガラス工芸家100人』(別冊炎芸術)、阿部出版、2021年

定期刊行物

- 「インタビュー No.27 池本一三さん」『工芸学会通信』No.79、財団法人工芸学会、1988年12月号
- 「グラス・ペインティングについて思うこと」『Glasswork a quarterly magazine on glass』No.8、株式会社アイデム・グラスワーク、1991年2月号
- シェグフライド・アーマン、矢野元子訳「池本一三の内面世界」『GLASS & ART』No.10、株式会社栄光、1995年8月号
- 池本一三「[連載]池本一三のやさしいフラット・ワーク学校」『GLASS & ART』No.14–21、株式会社栄光、1996年8月号–98年11月号 ＊第1回ドローイング、第2回《ステンドグラス技法》工具と制作工程、第3回《エナメル技法》材料と工程、第4回接着によるガラスの造形、第5回キルンワークの基礎知識、第6回キルンワークの基礎知識 II、第7回電気炉の仕組みと作り方、最終回作品を作るうえでの考え方
- 三島明子「感性のエナジー ガラス作家池本一三」『パトス』No.45、株式会社ポリッシュ・ワーク、2007年、
- 武田厚「拡張するガラスJAPAN 第27回現代に呼吸するガラス・作家論(2)」『美術の窓』No.483、株式会社生活の友社、2022年4月号

今井完眞 | Imai Sadamasa

1989 京都府生まれ
祖父・今井政之と父・今井眞正のもと、陶芸を学ぶ
2012 京都商工会議所インターンシップ交流事業の京都代表として、ベルナルド社(フランス・リモージュ)にて研修を受ける
2015 東京藝術大学大学院美術研究科陶芸専攻修了

1989 Born in Kyoto
Studies ceramics under his grandfather Imai Masayuki and father Imai Makimasa
2012 Undergoes training at Bernardaud (Limoges, France) as Kyoto representative on Kyoto Chamber of Commerce and Industry internship exchange program
2015 Completes master's program in ceramics at Tokyo University of the Arts

主な個展

2015 「今井完眞 個展」(銀座黒田陶苑／東京)['16–'20, '22, '23]
2016 「今井完眞 陶展—海—」(日本橋三越本店／東京)['20, '23]
2017 「—LIFE—今井完眞陶展」(大丸京都店)
2018 「今井完眞 陶展—1300℃の生命—」(日本橋三越本店アートスクエア／東京)
2019 「今井完眞 陶展」(そごう横浜店／神奈川)['22]
2020 「今井完眞 陶展」(福屋八丁堀本店／広島)
2021 「今井完眞展—強くそして速いもの—」(銀座黒田陶苑アネックス／東京)
「今井完眞 陶展」(松坂屋名古屋店／愛知)
2022 「—生き物のうつわ—今井完眞作陶展」(酒井京清堂／東京)

主なグループ展

2007 「京都市立銅駝美術工芸高等学校美工作品展」
2008 「竹原市主催 "竹原で育った陶芸家たち"」(たけはら美術館／京都)
2011 「男展」(東京藝術大学ギャラリー／東京)
「第1回中国高嶺国際陶芸展」(中国景徳鎮陶磁器博物館)
2012 「第49回杜窯会作陶展」(日本橋三越本店／東京)[第50回:2013、第52回:2015、第53回:2016]
2013 「SOTUTEN 2013」(代官山ヒルサイドテラス／東京)
「京焼・用の美展」(ケルン手工業会議所会館)
「京焼・美と創造展」(パリ日本文化会館)
「Japanese Contemporary Meets Tradition by Syota Nakatugawa and Sadamasa Imai」(MIZENKA GALLERY／東京)
「Small Strange Suits」(フリュウ・ギャラリー／東京)
「The 2013 International Symposium of Ceramics Art Education and Exchange」(トルコ)参加
「第8回 藝大アートプラザ大賞展」(東京藝術大学アートプラザ)
2014 「東京藝術大学陶芸研究室展」(東京藝術大学アートプラザ)
「アートフェア東京2014」(東京国際フォーラム)['15]
「—春来草自生—絵画と陶芸二人展」(銀座黒田陶苑／東京)
「歴史・町・広島竹原藝術祭 「藝術」、ですか?」(竹原市まちなみ保存地区／広島)
「京都歴代展—継承と展開」(京都市美術館)
2015 「東京藝術大学卒業・修了作品展」三菱地所賞
「新星展」(Artspace VISION 銀座／東京)
「第5回中、日、韓有名芸術家招待展」(Shanghai Art Collection Museum／上海)['16]
「現代作家茶碗展特集」(日本橋三越本店／東京)['16]
「藝大アーツイン丸の内2015」(丸ビル／東京)
「わん碗ONE展」(東五六／京都)
2016 「—伝承と創造— 陶芸家 今井政之三代展」(あべのハルカス近鉄本店／大阪)
2018 「今井政之・眞正・完眞陶展」(京都陶磁器会館)
「ゾクッとするリアリズム ゾウムシVSシーラカンス」展(茨城県立陶芸美術館)
2019 「いきもの狂騒曲—陶芸フィギュアの現在」展(茨城県立陶芸美術館)
「深井今井深井今井 四人の琳派 花鳥風月」(アトリエヒロ／大阪)
2020 「青か、白か、—青磁×白磁×青白磁—」(茨城県陶芸美術館)
2021 「京都府新鋭選抜展」(京都文化博物館)
2023 「真言宗立教開宗1200年記念 今井家三代特別展—未来に美をつなぐ—」(東寺小子房／京都)

主な受賞歴

2007 「京都市立銅駝美術工芸高等学校美工作品展」京都市教育長賞
2011 京都花鳥館賞奨学金 最優秀賞
2014 「「藝術」ですか? 歴史・町・広島芸術祭」青煉瓦賞(審査員賞)
2015 「東京藝術大学卒業・修了作品展」三菱地所賞
2021 「京都府新鋭選抜展」NHK京都放送局賞

展覧会図録

- 『第11回 筍豊会展』、ギャラリー101、2015年
- 『今井完眞陶展 海』、日本橋三越本店、2016年
- 『陶藝家今井政之三代展 伝承と創造』、あべのハルカス近鉄本店タワー館11階美術画廊、2016年
- 『文化功労者今井政之の藝術と今井家三代展 受けつがれる情熱』、福屋八丁堀本店8階催場、2017年
- 『今井完眞陶展 life』、大丸京都店6階美術画廊、2017年
- 『ゾクッとするリアリズム ゾウムシ VS シーラカンス』、茨城県陶芸美術館、2018年
- 『今井家三代展:生命(いのち)と炎のDNA』、阪神梅田本店9階美術画廊、2018年

- 『今井完眞陶展　1300℃の生命』、日本橋三越本店本館6階アートスクエア、2018年
- 『今井完眞個展　めでたい』、銀座黒田陶苑、2019年
- 『いきもの狂騒曲　陶芸フィギュアの現在』、茨城県陶芸美術館、2019年
- 『今井完眞陶展　土に遊ぶ』、そごう横浜店6階美術画廊、2019年
- 『ぐいのみ展　20周年企画』、ギャラリー数寄、2019年
- 『深井今井深井今井　四人の琳派　花鳥風月』、アトリエヒロ、2019年
- 『今井完眞陶展』、福屋八丁堀本店7階美術画廊、2020年
- 『今井完眞陶展　静中の動』、日本橋三越本店本館6階美術サロン、2020年
- 『香ノ器展　アトリエヒロ開廊五周年記念』、アトリエヒロ、2020年
- 『今井完眞 陶展』、そごう横浜店6階美術画廊、2022年

書籍

- 『陶芸家150人　2020年現代日本の精鋭たち』(別冊炎芸術)、阿部出版、2020年

定期刊行物

- 「「京焼」の新世紀」『炎芸術』No.127、阿部出版、2016年
- 岡田陽二、野田耕一「今井家三代、受け継がれる魂「土・炎・命」」『陶工房』No.82、誠文堂新光社、2016年9月号
- 「世界を「アッ」と言わせる、手わざとカタチ!!「超・立体」アートとしての最新工芸」『月刊美術』No.497、サン・アート、2017年2月号
- 「新世代15作家の「用の美」」『月刊美術』No.513、サン・アート、2018年6月号
- 梶山博史「やきものである必然性—今井完眞の造形」『炎芸術』No.146、阿部出版、2021年5月号
- 「悠久のひととき Vol.176: 陶芸家 今井完眞」『極上の休日』、西武そごう、2022年11月号

WEB

- 『今井完眞 official』(http://sadamasa-imai.jp/biography.html)[2022年12月26日最終アクセス]
- 「陶芸家・今井完眞さんがつくる海洋生物がリアルすぎる！ 制作へのこだわりや工房を紹介」『和楽web』(https://intojapanwaraku.com/craft/69267/)[2022年12月26日最終アクセス]

植葉香澄 | Ueba Kasumi

1978 京都府生まれ
2003 京都府陶工高等技術専門校図案科修了

1978 Born in Kyoto
2003 Completes studies in design at Kyoto Prefectural Technical College of Ceramic Arts

主な個展
2006 「植葉香澄展」(SAVOIR VIVRE Store&Gallery／東京)[-'08, '13, '16-'19, '22]
「植葉香澄展」(ギャラリー器館／京都)
2014 「植葉香澄展 キメラがやってきた!」(髙島屋京都店6階美術画廊・日本橋髙島屋6階美術画廊／東京)
2018 「植葉香澄 キメラエボリューション」(日本橋髙島屋美術画廊／東京ほか)
2020 「植葉香澄」(館・游彩/東京)
2021 「植葉香澄展―宝尽くして春を待つ」(日本橋髙島屋美術画廊／東京ほか)

主なグループ展
2008 「京都府美術工芸新鋭展 京都工芸ビエンナーレ」(京都文化博物館)
「第3回パラミタ陶芸大賞展」(パラミタミュージアム／三重)
2009 「現代工芸作家がつくる未来へのタカラモノ」(髙島屋東京店6階美術画廊ほか)
「現代工芸への視点―装飾の力」展(東京国立近代美術館工芸館)
2014 「現代美術工芸の新しい地平Part I 漆と陶―素材を超えて」(渋谷ヒカリエ8／東京)
「現代・陶芸現象」(茨城県陶芸美術館)
2015 「琳派400年記念 新鋭選抜展」(京都文化博物館)
「進行形女子陶芸」(茨城県陶芸美術館)['17]
2016 「Revalue Nippon Project 展」(パナソニック汐留美術館/ 東京)
「現代陶芸・案内(ガイド)」(茨城県陶芸美術館)
2017 「かわいいやきものわきあいあい」(兵庫陶芸美術館)
「現代の茶陶」(茨城県陶芸美術館)
2018 「春爛漫―ポップ＆モダン」(アートフロントギャラリー／東京)
2019 「京 区区たる九人展」(柿傳ギャラリー／東京)

主な受賞歴
2011 京都府文化賞奨励賞
2012 京都市芸術新人賞
2015 「琳派400年記念 新鋭選抜展」毎日新聞社賞

展覧会図録
- 『装飾の力』、東京国立近代美術館、2009年
- 『現代工芸作家がつくる未来へのタカラモノ』、髙島屋東京店6階美術画廊ほか、2009年
- 『植葉香澄展 キメラがやってきた!』、髙島屋京都店6階美術画廊・日本橋髙島屋6階美術画廊、2014年
- 『現代・陶芸現象』、茨城県陶芸美術館、2014年
- 『進行形女子陶芸』、茨城県陶芸美術館、2015年
- 『現代陶芸・案内』、茨城県陶芸美術館、2016年
- 『Revalue Nippon project 中田英寿が出会った日本工芸』、パナソニック汐留美術館、2016年
- 『現代の茶陶』、茨城県陶芸美術館、2017年
- 『春爛漫 ポップ＆モダン』、Art Front Gallery、2019年
- 『京 区区たる九人展』、柿傳ギャラリー、2019年
- 『植葉香澄展 宝尽くして春を待つ』、髙島屋日本橋本店6階美術画廊ほか、2021年

書籍
- 『陶芸家150人 2020年現代日本の精鋭たち』(別冊炎芸術)、阿部出版、2020年

定期刊行物
- 『目の眼 古美術・民芸のこころにふれる』No.373、里文出版、2007年10月号
- 柴辻政彦「植葉香澄―奇想の陶芸「キメラ」」『陶説』No.685、日本陶磁協会、2010年4月号
- 「イケテル陶芸 熱くてクールな、未来の千両役者たち」『月刊美術』No.431、サン・アート、2011年8月号
- 「気鋭作家60人の"たなごころの美"」『月刊美術』No.459、サン・アート、2013年12月号
- 「「京焼」の新世紀」『炎芸術』No.127、阿部出版、2016年8月号
- 「今、注目の陶芸家30人」『炎芸術』No.129、阿部出版、2017年2月号

桂盛仁｜Katsura Morihito

1944 東京都生まれ
1966 武蔵野美術短期大学にてグラフィックデザインを学ぶ
1992 伊勢神宮の式年遷宮に参加、御神宝を制作
2008 重要無形文化財「彫金」保持者認定
伊勢神宮の式年遷宮に参加、御神宝を制作
2011 文化庁からの依頼を受け、《天道虫小金具制作工程見本》を制作
2013 紺綬褒章受章
2015 旭日小綬章受章
2018 奈良薬師寺国宝東塔の舎利容器を制作
2021 紺綬褒章受章
2022 春日大社若宮神社の式年造替に参加、国宝・御神宝《金鶴洲浜台》・《銀鶴及磯形》を復元制作

1944 Born in Tokyo
1966 Studies graphic design at Musashino Art University Junior College of Art and Design
1992 Makes sacred objects for the Shikinen Sengū ritual rebuilding of Ise Grand Shrine
2008 Recognized as holder of important intangible cultural property for *chokin*
Makes sacred objects for the Shikinen Sengu ritual rebuilding of Ise Grand Shrine
2011 Commissioned by the Agency for Cultural Affairs to produce "Samples illustrating production processes for a small clasp with ladybug design"
2013 Receives Medal with Dark Blue Ribbon
2015 Receives The Order of the Rising Sun, Gold Rays with Rosette
2018 Makes relics box for the Eastern Pagoda (national treasure) at Yakushiji temple in Nara
2021 Receives Medal with Dark Blue Ribbon
2022 Takes part in ritual rebuilding of Wakamiya Shrine, Kasuga Taisha (Nara), working on replicas of national treasures depicting "Gold Cranes on Sandy Beach Stands" and "Silver Cranes on Shoreline Stands"

主な個展

1987 個展（渋谷ぎゃらりいすぎ山／東京）
2006 「桂盛仁彫金の世界」（日本橋三越本店／東京）
2009 人間国宝認定記念個展「人間国宝―桂盛仁　彫金の世界」（日本橋三越本店／東京）
2013 「人間国宝―桂盛仁 彫金の世界―」（三越大阪店）
「人間国宝　桂盛仁展」（宮本商行／東京）
2016 「桂盛行・盛仁父子展」（奈良薬師寺）
2018 「人間国宝・桂盛仁金工の世界」（練馬区立美術館／東京）
2022 「桂盛仁展―命の輝きを謳う―」（間 AWAI THE COVER NIPPON／東京）

主なグループ展

1971 「第1回伝統工芸日本金工展」[–'22]
1988 「小品展」（日本橋三越本店／東京）
1994 「第2回全日本金・銀創作展」
「第45回日本伝統工芸展」
2004 「現代の「日本の金工」展」（デンマーク王立工芸博物館／コペンハーゲン）
2010 「日本伝統工芸会東日本支部50周年記念展」（MOA美術館／静岡）
2011 「「日本のわざと美」展―重要無形文化財とそれを支える人々―」（島根県立石見美術館ほか）[–'18]
「神宮奉納美術―心とかたち―VII」（式年遷宮記念神宮美術館／三重）
2012 「伝統工芸の匠」特別展（パレスホテル東京／東京）
2013 「人間国宝小品展」（日本橋三越本店／東京）
「燕手仕事展」（燕市産業資料館／新潟）
2014 「人間国宝の現在（いま）」（東京国立博物館／東京）
「美の創造者たち」（神宮美術館／三重）
「人間国宝展」（MOA美術館／静岡）
「静―歌会始御題によせて―」（式年遷宮記念神宮美術館／三重）
2016 「工芸・Kogeiの創造―人間国宝展―」（銀座和光／東京）
2018 特別展「金属工芸」（金沢市立安江金箔工芸館／石川）
2021 「Japan: A History of Style」（メトロポリタン美術館／ニューヨーク）
2022 「岩田広己・桂盛仁・小林誠 3人展」（アートスペース煌翔／東京）
式年造替記念特別展「春日大社　若宮国宝展」（奈良国立博物館）
2023 「薬師寺国宝東塔大修理落慶記念　現代作家による白鳳時代から目覚めた作品達展」（日本橋三越本店／東京）

主な受賞歴

1975 「第5回伝統工芸日本金工展」奨励賞[第7回：1977、第8回：1978]
1994 「第2回全日本金・銀創作展」委員会会長賞
1995 「第25回伝統工芸日本金工展」文化庁長官賞
1998 「第28回伝統工芸日本金工展」日本工芸会賞
「第45回日本伝統工芸展」東京都知事賞
2009 公益財団法人宗桂会　宗桂会大賞

展覧会図録

- 『人間国宝　桂 盛仁　彫金の世界』、日本橋三越本店、2006年[2012年]
- 『静　歌会始御題によせて』、式年遷宮記念神宮美術館、2014年
- 『工芸・Kôgeiの創造　人間国宝展』、銀座和光、2016年
- 『人間国宝・桂盛仁金工の世界　江戸彫金の技』、練馬区立美術館、2018年
- 『金属工芸』、金沢市立安江金箔工芸館、2018年
- 『式年造替記念特別展　春日大社　若宮国宝展』、奈良国立博物館、2022年

書籍

- 桂盛仁『超技法・桂盛仁の彫金』、株式会社芸艸堂、2018年

定期刊行物

- 「てんとう虫の装身具　桂盛仁」『Jewel：mode & art』No.351、レーヌ出版、2004年
- 「「彫金金具制作工程について」桂盛仁／工芸探訪シリーズ（18）」『宗桂会だより　加賀象嵌を次の世代に』No.27、宗桂会、2010年
- 「和装／日本ジュウリーデザイナー協会45周年記念／つくるひと・インタビュー　桂盛仁―2009」『Jewel：mode & art』No.414、レーヌ出版、2009年
- 「人間国宝の肖像（3）桂盛仁×小山薫堂」『Pen』No.424、TBSブリタニカ、2017年
- 「失われゆく技と美[桂盛仁]」『Centurion』、Winter 2018、ミュンヘン：ジャーナル・インターナショナル・エクスペリエンス、2018年
- 「《人間国宝・桂盛仁　金工の世界—江戸彫金の技》」『Jewel：mode & art』No.501、レーヌ出版、2019年
- 「春日若宮式年造替　金鶴洲浜台調進」『皇室』No.94（春）、扶桑社、2022年

その他

- 『彫金―桂盛仁のわざ―』（伝統工芸技術記録映画シリーズ）、文化庁、2010年

桑田卓郎 | Kuwata Takuro

1981 広島県生まれ
2001 京都嵯峨芸術大学短期大学部美術学科陶芸コース卒業
2002 陶芸家・財満進氏に師事
2007 多治見市陶磁器意匠研究所修了

1981 Born in Hiroshima Prefecture
2001 Graduates from ceramics course at Kyoto Saga University of Arts, Department of Fine Arts, Ceramic Arts
2002 Apprenticeship under master ceramicist Zaima Susumu
2007 Completes studies at Tajimi City Pottery Design and Technical Center

主な個展

2008 「TETSUKI」(銀座黒田陶苑/東京)['09-'11, '13, '15, '19]
2010 「桑田卓郎展」(小山登美夫ギャラリー/東京)
個展(ギャラリーMITATE/東京)
「桑田卓郎展」(画廊 光芳堂/岐阜)['14, '21]
2012 「CUP」(柿傳ギャラリー/東京)['15, '18, '20]
2013 「ZUNGURIMUKKURI」(Salon 94/ニューヨーク)['15, '21]
2014 「From Nature」(Pierre Marie Giraud/ブリュッセル)
「Hi Tea Bowl, I'm in Paris」(Pierre Marie Giraud/パリ)['17, '19, '20]
2015 「天国」(草月会館1F石庭/東京)
「桑田卓郎展」(8/ ART GALLERY/ Tomio Koyama Gallery/東京)['13]
2016 「From Tea Bowl」(Alison Jacques Gallery/ロンドン)
2017 「Good Morning, Tea Bowl」(Pierre Marie Giraud/ブリュッセル)
「TEE BOWL」(KOSAKU KANECHIKA/東京)['21]
2018 「Are You Going Out, Tea Bowl?」(Galeria Mascota/メキシコ)
「TAKURO KUWATA meets Trading Museum COMME des GARÇONS」(Trading Museum COMME des GARÇONS/東京)
2019 「Dear Tea Bowl, Horsetails are in season in Hagi.」(山口県立萩美術館・浦上記念館)
「日々」(音羽山清水寺/京都)
「today」(Pierre Marie Giraud/ブリュッセル)
2021 「湯呑」(ROPPONGI HILLS A/D GALLERY/東京)
「USE」(Roll/東京)
2022 「桑田卓郎展」(銀座 蔦屋書店/東京)
「Dancing Udon」(THE GALLERY/ニューヨーク)

主なグループ展

2010 「カラー やきものと色の密かな関係」(岐阜県現代陶芸美術館)
2011 「東海現代陶芸 思考する新世代展」(愛知県陶芸資料館)
「Paul Clay」(Salon 94 Bowery/ニューヨーク)
2012 「工芸未来派」(金沢21世紀美術館/石川)
「第7回 パラミタ陶芸大賞展」(パラミタミュージアム/三重)
2013 「Ceramic Sculpture」(Rhona Hoffman Gallery/シカゴ)
「10 Under 40」(ISTANBUL'74/イスタンブール)
「現代の名碗」(菊池寛実記念 智美術館/東京)
2014 「More Material」(Salon 94 Bowery/ニューヨーク)
「現代・陶芸現象」(茨城県陶芸美術館)
「FIRE!」(Venus Manhattan/ニューヨーク)
2015 「Wabi Sabi Shima」(Thalie Art Foundation/ブリュッセル)
「2732: Try Again. Fail Again. Fail Better」(Cherry and Martin/ロサンゼルス)
「Japanese Kōgei | Future Forward」(Museum of Arts and Design/ニューヨーク)
「Come after Magic」(aura gallery taipei/台北)
2016 「PUNK 工芸—魂の救済」(樂翠亭美術館/富山)
2017 「村上隆のスーパーフラット現代陶芸考」(十和田市現代美術館/青森)
「MIDTOWN」(Lever House/ニューヨーク)
「Frieze Sculpture 2017」(Regent's Park/ロンドン)
「茶陶の現在—2018萩」(山口県立萩美術館・浦上記念館)
2018 「Fire and Clay」(Gagosian Gallery/ジュネーブ)
「バブルラップ」(熊本市現代美術館)
2019 「CERAMIC MOMENTUM—Staging the Object」(CLAY Museum of Ceramic Art/デンマーク)
「現在地:未来の地図を描くために[2]」(金沢21世紀美術館/石川)
2020 「世界は今:アートとつながる」(金沢21世紀美術館/石川)
「近代陶芸 陶芸家たちの古典復興」(ポーラ美術館/神奈川)
「和巧絶佳—令和時代の超工芸」(パナソニック汐留美術館/東京ほか)
2021 「The Flames: The Age of Ceramics」(パリ市立近代美術館)
「豊かなる茶陶」(茨城県陶芸美術館)
2022 「Dear Friend」(KOSAKU KANECHIKA/東京)
「ホモ・ファーベルの断片—人とものづくりの未来—」(愛知県陶磁美術館)
「ロマンティック・プログレス」(岐阜県現代陶芸美術館)
「Strange Clay: Ceramics in Contemporary Art」(Hayward Gallery/ロンドン)

主な受賞歴

2006「第6回益子陶芸展」濱田庄司賞
2007「第2回織部クラフト・デザイン大賞」銀賞
2008「第8回国際陶磁器展美濃」美濃賞
「第26回朝日現代クラフト展」奨励賞
2009「テーブルウェアフェスティバル2009」第17回テーブルウェア大賞グランプリ・経済産業大臣賞
2018「Loewe Craft Prize 2018」特別賞
2022 日本陶磁器協会賞

展覧会図録

- 『Takuro Kuwata from nature』、Pierre Marie Giraud、2015年
- 『桑田卓郎 I'm home, tea bowl』、Kosaku Kanechika、2018年

書籍

- 秋元雄史『工芸未来派：アート化する新しい工芸』、六耀社、2016年
- 『C CÉRAMIQUES JAPONAISES CONTEMPORAINES』、iKi édition、2016年
- VITAMIN C『CLAY + CERAMIC』、Phaidon Press、2017年
- 山本浩貴『ポスト人新世の芸術』、美術出版社、2022年

定期刊行物

- 『apartamento magazine』No.23 、APARTAMENTO、2019年
- 「Live Your Color」『Numéro TOKYO』No.133、扶桑社、2020年
- 『PURPLE』No.34、Purple Institute、2020年
- 「2021年度日本陶磁協会賞・金賞受賞記念 桑田卓郎・三島喜美代展」『陶説』、No.833、日本陶磁協会、2022年11月号

小宮康義 | Komiya Yasuyoshi

1982 東京都生まれ
2004 大学進学とともに祖父・小宮康孝、父・小宮康正に師事し、江戸小紋の技術を習得
2008 東京造形大学絵画専攻領域卒業

1982 Born in Tokyo
2004 At the same time as entering university, begins studies of *Edo komon* kimono techniques under his grandfather Komiya Yasutaka and father Komiya Yasumasa
2008 Graduates from Tokyo Zokei University, with a painting major

主なグループ展

2011 開館20周年記念展「江戸小紋を伝える　小宮家のわざと人」(葛飾区郷土と天文の博物館/東京)
2015 「今に生きる江戸小紋」(シルク博物館/神奈川)
2017 「第64回日本伝統工芸展」(日本橋三越本店/東京ほか)[第68回:2021年]
2018 「第52回日本伝統工芸染織展」(日本橋三越本店/東京ほか)[第55回:2021年]
2022 「第3回日本を継ぐ—工芸作家、くらしのしつらえ—」(丸善日本橋店3階ギャラリー/東京)

主な受賞歴

2017 「第64回日本伝統工芸展」日本工芸会奨励賞[第68回:2021]
2018 「第52回日本伝統工芸染織展」三越伊勢丹賞
2021 「第55回日本伝統工芸染織展」奨励賞・三越伊勢丹賞

展覧会図録

- 『開館20周年記念展　江戸小紋を伝える　小宮家のわざと人』、葛飾区郷土と天文の博物館、2011年

定期刊行物

- 小宮康孝、大滝幹夫「対談　型紙、型染め—伝統工芸への思い」『日本の美術12』No.343、至文堂、1994年12月号

WEB

- 「#029　東京都　江戸小紋職人　小宮康義」『明日への扉』(https://www.athome-tobira.jp/story/029-komiya-yasuyoshi.html)[2022年12月27日最終アクセス]

その他

- 菊池理予「工芸技術記録に関する研究—『江戸小紋技術記録』を通じて—」『無形文化遺産部プロジェクト報告書　無形文化財の伝承に関する資料集』、独立行政法人国立文化財機構東京文化財研究所無形文化遺産部、2011年
- 水上嘉代子「江戸小紋の美—小宮家の技術—」『東京造形大学研究報』No.21、東京造形大学、2020年

城間栄市 | Shiroma Eiichi

1977 沖縄県生まれ
紅型宗家15代である父・城間栄順に師事
2003 インドネシア・ジョグジャカルタにてバティックを学ぶ(–2004)
2018 「城間びんがた工房」代表

1977 Born in Okinawa Prefecture
Apprenticeship under his father, Shiroma Eijun, 15th generation *bingata* master artisan
2003 Studies batik in Yogyakarta, Indonesia (until 2004)
2018 Takes over as head of Shiroma Bingata Workshop

主なグループ展

2000 「第52回沖展」(浦添市民体育館／沖縄)[第55回：'03、第60回：'08、第62–64回：'10–'12]
「工芸王国—きらめく手わざの世界を沖縄から」(沖縄県立博物館)
2001 「工芸王国　人・技・心」(沖縄県立博物館)
2011 「第58回日本伝統工芸展」(三越名古屋栄店／愛知ほか)
「第45回日本工芸会染織展」(大丸京都店ほか)
2012 「第47回西部伝統工芸展」(福岡三越・鶴屋百貨店／熊本)[第49回：'14、第55回：'21]
2015 「城間家の仕事　三代継承展」(沖縄県立博物館・美術館ほか)
「第62回日本伝統工芸展」(日本橋三越本店／東京ほか)
2022 城間栄順米寿記念「紅(いろ)の衣」(沖縄県立博物館・美術館ほか)
「明日の工藝　第22回岡田茂吉賞」(MOA美術館／静岡)

主な受賞歴

2003 「第55回沖展」奨励賞[第60回：'08、第62回：'10]
2011 「第63回沖展」沖展賞
2012 「第64回沖展」準会員賞
2012 「第47回西部伝統工芸展」福岡市長賞
2014 「第49回西部伝統工芸展」奨励賞
2015 「第62回日本伝統工芸展」日本工芸会新人賞
2016 第50回沖縄タイムス芸術選賞奨励賞
2021 「第55回西部伝統工芸展」沖縄タイムス社賞
2022 第22回岡田茂吉賞大賞

展覧会図録

- 『工芸王国—きらめく手わざの世界を沖縄から』、沖縄県立博物館、2000年
- 『工芸王国 人・技・心 企画展』、沖縄県立博物館、2001年

定期刊行物

- 「知っておきたい染織作家ガイド　活躍中の染織作家100名を総まとめ(別冊付録)」『美しいキモノ』No.255、婦人画報社、2016年

WEB

- 『日本工芸会ホームページ』(https://www.nihonkogeikai.or.jp/)[2023年1月4日最終アクセス]
- 『銀座もとじホームページ』(https://www.motoji.co.jp/blogs/artists-origins/shiromaeiichi)[2023年1月4日最終アクセス]
- 『NIHONMONO「にほん」の「ほんもの」を巡る旅マガジン』(https://nihonmono.jp/article/22592/)[2023年1月4日最終アクセス]
- 「城間びんがた工房　16代目・城間栄市×やまと　代表取締役社長・矢嶋孝行　スペシャル対談」『やまと』(https://www.kimono-yamato.co.jp/articles/shiroma_bingata_interview/)[2023年1月4日最終アクセス]
- 「会員・準会員紹介　城間栄市」『沖展オフィシャルサイト』(https://okiten.okinawatimes.co.jp/cms/member/dyeing/post2329/)[2023年1月18日最終アクセス]

須藤玲子 | Sudo Reiko

1953 茨城県生まれ
1975 武蔵野美術短期大学工芸デザイン学部専攻科修了
武蔵野美術大学造形学部工芸工業デザイン学科テキスタイル研究室助手(–1977)
1984 株式会社「布」設立に参加、現在は同社取締役デザインディレクター
2004 UCA芸術大学(イギリス)より名誉修士号授与
2007 東京造形大学デザイン学科教授、現在名誉教授(2019–)
2016 セントラル・セント・マーチンズ(ロンドン)客員教授(–現在)

1953 Born in Ibaraki Prefecture
1975 Completes studies with major in craft design at Musashino Art University Junior College of Art and Design
Research assistant in textiles, Department of Industrial Interior and Craft Design, Musashino Art University (until 1997)
1984 Co-founds Nuno Corporation. Currently serves as Design Director
2004 Receives honorary doctorate from University for the Creative Arts (UK)
2007 Becomes professor in Design Department at Tokyo Zokei University. (Professor emerita since 2019).
2016 Visiting professor at Central Saint Martins, University of the Arts, London (ongoing)

主な個展

2001 「布・技と術 NUNO-Sense and Skill」(京都芸術センターほか)[–'03]
2002 「Tradition and Innovation-Contemporary Textiles from the NUNO studio」(UCLAファウラー美術館/ロサンゼルスほか)
2004 「センス&スキル」(スヴェンスクホルム/ストックホルムほか)
2005 「2121: the textile vision of Reiko Sudo and nuno」(ジェイムズ・ホッキーギャラリー/イギリスほか)
2007 「NUNO Japanese Tradition Innovation Cloth」(ボルチモア美術館/アメリカほか)
2008 「NUNO・kibiso 須藤玲子展」(ギャラリーanima/大阪)
「Japan! Culture + Hyperculture」(ジョン・F・ケネディ舞台芸術センター/ワシントンD.C.)
2009 「Tokyo 101– Nuno textile by Reiko Sudo」(ノルデイックハウス/アイスランドほか)
2011 2011 KAUNAS Biennial「Reiko Sudo + NUNO「Rewind –Play-Forward」(国立チュルリョーニス美術館/リトアニア)
2012 「Japanese Style: Sustaining Design, Nuno「ZOKU ZOKU」」(ルーシン・クラフトセンター/イギリスほか)
2013 「Do You Nuno? 須藤玲子とNunoの世界」(松屋銀座7階デザインギャラリー1953/東京)['15:グランビスタギャラリーサッポロ/札幌、'17:ファイバースペースギャラリー/ストックホルム]
2014 「Reiko Sudo and Nuno: Textiles from Japan」(ミシシッピ・ヴァレー・テキスタイルミュージアム/カナダ)
「Koi Current」(フランス国立ギメ東洋美術館/パリ)
「なに NUNO ね?展」(ギャラリー ル・ベイン/東京)
2015 「2015 HANCOCK FELLOW: REIKO SUDO」(オーストラリア タペストリーワークショップ/メルボルン)
ITCC 2015「プレイフル・ビジョン:NUNOの布づくり」(マルマラ大学ジュホーリーイェット美術館/イスタンブール)
2016 「Scraps: Fashion, Textiles, and Creative Reuse」(クーパーヒューイット・スミソニアン・デザイン博物館/ニューヨークほか)
「Tradition and Innovation-Contemporary Textiles from the NUNO studio」(UCLAファウラー美術館/ロサンゼルスほか)
2017 「Fantasy in Japan Blue」(ジョン・F・ケネディ舞台芸術センター/ワシントンD.C.)
「NunoZokuScarves」(ルティン・クラフト・センター/イギリス)
「Coded Threads Textiles & Technology」(ウエスタンギャラリー/ワシントン)
2018 「織り道シルクロード布地美術」(敦煌研究院/中国)
2019 「NUNO—現代を生きる布の詩(うた)」(ジャパン・ハウス/サンパウロ)
「Making Nuno Japanese Textile Innovation from Sudo Reiko」(CHAT; Centre for Heritage, Arts and Textile/香港)['21:ジャパン・ハウス/ロンドンほか]
2021 「北陸工芸の祭典GO FOR KOGEI 2021 "扇の舞2021"」(勝興寺/富山)
作品集『NUNO—Visionary Japanese Textiles』刊行記念「nuno nuno」展(AXISギャラリー/東京)
「松ヶ岡開墾150周特別展示 サーキュラー・デザイン—kibisoはつづく—」(松ヶ岡開墾場 二番蚕室二階/山形)
2022 「SUDŌ REIKO—MAKING NUNO TEXTILE INNOVATION AUS JAPAN」(Textilmuseum St.Gallen/スイス)
「堀川新文化ビルヂング会館1周記念"KYOTO nuno nuno"」(堀川新文化ビルチング/京都)
「酒井家庄内入部400記念事業 NUNOとwe+によるテキスタイルインスタレーション"ファンファーレ 扇の舞"」(鶴岡アートフォーラム/山形)

主なグループ展

1977 「テキスタイル展」(アート川島/東京)
1984 「テキスタイル・アクセサリーズ」(サボア・ピープル/東京)
1986 「ジャパン・クリエイティブ」(西武百貨店/東京)
「Color, Light, Surface」(クーパー・ヒューイット国立デザイン博物館/ニューヨーク)['94:京都産業センター]
1994 「2010-Textiles and New Technology」(クラフト・カウンシル・ギャラリー/ロンドン)
「Japanese Design-A Survery since 1950」(フィラデルフィア美術館/アメリカほか)
1995 「Runway Show of Japanese Fashion」(ノースダコタ州立美術館/アメリカ)
「NUNO: Japnanese Textiles for the Body」(オレゴン美術館/アメリカ)
1996 「TEXTILE MAGICIAN「(イスラエル美術館/エルサレム)
1998 「Structure and Surface: Contemporary Japanese Textile」(ニューヨーク近代美術館ほか)[–'01]
2000 「Design World 2000展」(アート&デザイン美術館/ヘルシンキ)
2001 「Tradition and Innovation: Contemporary Textiles by NUNO Studio,Tokyo」(カリフォルニア大学サンタバーバラ校美術館ほか)
「現代の布 染と織の造形思考」(東京国立近代美術館工芸館)
2003 「Beyond the Surface: Japanese Style of Making Things」(シンガポール美術館ほか)[–'04]
2005 「2121: The textile vision of Reiko Sudo and Nuno」(ハンブルグ美術工芸博物館/ドイツほか)[–'07]
「素材×技術からフォルムへ・布と金属展」(茨城県つくば美術館)

2007 「Design de sign 須藤玲子＋眞田岳彦」（桑沢デザイン研究所／東京）
「〈素材×技術〉からフォルムへ―布と金属」（茨城県つくば美術館）
2010 「National Design Triennial: Why Design Now?」（クーパー・ヒューイット国立デザイン博物館／ニューヨーク）
2011 「Lost in Lace」（バーミンガム美術館／イギリス）
「Playful Vision: Reiko sudo and NunoTextile Images」（M.K.チョルリョーニス国立美術館／リトアニア）
2012 「Japanese Style-Sustaining Design」（ルーシン・クラフトセンター／イギリス）
2013 「現代のプロダクトデザイン―Made in Japanを生む展」（東京国立近代美術館）［-'14］
2014 「コイ・カレント展」（フランス国立ギメ東洋美術館／パリ）
2016 「伝統の未来展」（松屋銀座／東京）
2017 「素材と対話するアートとデザイン展」（富山県美術館）
「交わるいと「あいだ」をひらく術として展」（広島市現代美術館）［-'18］
2018 「いばらき工芸大全Ⅲ 染織の巻"展"」（茨城県陶芸美術館）
「こいのぼりなう！ 須藤玲子×アドリアン・ガルデール×齋藤精一によるインスタレーション」（国立新美術館／東京）
「アート＆デザインの大茶会 マルセル・ワンダース、須藤玲子、ミヤケマイ：踊るこいのぼり 須藤玲子×アドリアン・ガルデールによるインスタレーション」（大分県立美術館展示室A）
2019 「㊙めったに見られないデザイナーたちの原画」（21_21 DESIGN SIGHTギャラリー1＆2／東京）
2020 「パッション20 さわってプリーズ NUNOの布づくり」（東京国立近代美術館工芸館内 休憩室）
「Kimono: Kyoto to Catwalk」（ヴィクトリア＆アルバート博物館／ロンドン）
「FABRIC: TOUCH & IDENTITY「Ogi no mai/ Japanese Fanfare 2020」」（コンプトンバーニー ギャラリーアンドパーク／イギリス）
「6つの個展 2020」（茨城県近代美術館）
2021 「北陸工芸の祭典GO FOR KOGEI 2021 "扇の舞2021"」（勝興寺／富山）
2022 「DESIGN MUSEUM JAPAN展 集めてつなごう 日本のデザイン」（国立新美術館 企画展示室1E／ 東京）
2023 「第11回円空大賞展 共鳴―継続と創造」（岐阜県美術館）

主な受賞歴

1994 ロスコー賞（クーパー・ヒューイット・ナショナルデザインミュージアム／アメリカ）
1999 JID賞部門賞（日本インテリアデザイナー協会）
2006 桑沢学園賞（学校法人桑沢学園）
2006 第52回毎日デザイン賞（毎日新聞社）
2022 第11回円空大賞（岐阜県）

展覧会図録

- 『現代の布：染と織の造形思考』、東京国立近代美術館、2001年
- 『布・技と術／ぬの・わざとわざ』、京都芸術センター、2001年
- 『21:21―The Textile Vision of Reiko Sudo and Nuno』、ジェイムズ・ホッキー・ギャラリーほか、2005年
- 『Japan!：culture ＋ hyperculture』、ジョン・F・ケネディ舞台芸術センター、2008年
- 『現代のプロダクトデザイン―Made in Japanを生む』、東京国立近代美術館、2013年
- 『Scraps: Fashion, Textiles, and Creative Reuse』、クーパー・ヒューイット・スミソニアン・デザイン博物館ほか、2016年
- 『こいのぼりなう！ 須藤玲子×アドリアン・ガルデール×齋藤精一によるインスタレーション』、国立新美術館、2018年
- 『6つの個展 2020』、茨城県近代美術館、2020年

書籍

- 『NUNO NUNO BOOKS：SUKESUKE』、NUNO、1997年
- 『NUNO NUNO BOOKS：BOROBORO』、NUNO、1997年
- 『NUNO NUNO BOOKS：FUAFUWA』、NUNO、1998年
- 『NUNO NUNO BOOKS：SHIMIJIMI』、NUNO、1998年
- 『NUNO NUNO BOOKS：KIRAKIRA』、NUNO、1999年
- 『NUNO NUNO BOOKS：ZAWAZAWA』、NUNO、1999年
- 『NUNO NUNO BOOKS：ZOKUZOKU』、NUNO、2012年
- 『透けるトート 工芸館開館30周年記念』、東京国立近代美術館、2007年
- 『Nunoトレイ 工芸館開館30周年記念』、東京国立近代美術館、2007年
- 『工芸館名品集―染織 』、東京国立近代美術館、2009年
- 須藤玲子『日本の布1』、良品計画、2018年
- 須藤玲子『日本の布2』、良品計画、2018年
- 須藤玲子『日本の布3』、良品計画、2019年
- 須藤玲子『日本の布4』、良品計画、2019年
- 『NUNO―Visionary Japanese Textiles』、Thames & Hudson、2021年

定期刊行物

- 「表裏のない布」『GA JAPAN』No.52、A.D.A.EDITA Tokyo、2001年9月号
- 「さまざまなコラボレーションを通して」『新建築』No.52、新建築社、2001年12月号
- 「NUNOの布づくり」『染織α』No.243、染織と生活社、2001年6月号
- 「NUNOの布づくり（連載エッセイ）」『日本繊維新聞』、日本繊維新聞社、2009年5-7月号
- 「自然とファッション」『Earth Winds』、SOMARS、2010年10月号

田口義明 | Taguchi Yoshiaki

1958 東京都生まれ
1977 父・田口善国に師事し、蒔絵の技術を習得
1978 増村益城に師事し、髹漆の技術を習得
1990 天皇高御座制作に参加
1991 伊勢神宮御神宝制作に参加
1996 国宝《梅蒔絵手箱》復元模造制作に参加
2008 紫綬褒章
2022 「日本工芸会×飛鳥クルーズ(飛鳥II)」に参加

1958 Born in Tokyo
1977 Apprenticeship studying *maki-e* lacquerware techniques under his father, Taguchi Yoshikuni
1978 Apprenticeship studying *kyushitsu* lacquerware techniques under lacquerware master Masumura Mashiki
1990 Part of team of artisans making ceremonial throne (*takamikura*) for Japanese emperor
1991 Makes sacred objects for Ise Grand Shrine
1996 Helps to make replica of national treasure "*Ume makie tebako*" (Cosmetics box with plum *makie* lacquerwork)
2008 Receives Medal with Purple Ribbon
2022 Contributed pieces to Japan Kogei Association × Asuka Cruise

主なグループ展

1985 「第32回日本伝統工芸展」(日本橋三越本店/東京ほか)
1996 「虹色の漆 現代の美展」(ニューヨークジャパンソサイエティーギャラリー・デンバー美術館/アメリカ)
2000 「漆の美展」(東京都美術館ギャラリー/東京)['02, '08, '18, '23]
2001 「九つの音色展」(日本橋三越本店/東京)['03–'07,'20]
2002 「Japanese Crafts: Materials and Way of Formative Thinking」(インドネシア国立美術館/インドネシア・ペトロナス・ギャラリー/マレーシア)
2003 「わざの美 日本伝統工芸展50年記念展」(日本橋三越本店/東京ほか)
2006 「JAPAN & KOREA 漆 arts」(東京藝術大学大学美術館・石川県輪島漆芸美術館)
2007 開館30年記念展「工芸の力 21世紀の展望」(東京国立近代美術館工芸館)
2008 「ヌーベル・エル 美の今日展」(日本橋三越本店/東京)
2009 特別展「—生—歌会始御題に寄せて—」(式年遷宮記念神宮美術館/三重)
2010 特別展「—光—歌会始御題に寄せて—」(式年遷宮記念神宮美術館/三重)
特別展「21世紀の伝統工芸展—世界の眼—」(MOA美術館/静岡)
2012 「寿ぎのうつわ展」(東京国立近代美術館工芸館)
2013 「日本伝統工芸展60回記念 工芸からKŌGEIへ」(東京国立近代美術館工芸館)
「現代の日本工芸展 Contemporary KŌGEI Styles in Japan」(森上博物館/アメリカ)
2014 「Beauty of KOGEI Art Crafts in Japan「わざの美—日本の工芸」」(ジャパン・クリエイティブ・センター/シンガポール)
「第19回MOA岡田茂吉賞 明日の工芸を展望する」(MOA美術館/静岡)
2015 「菊池寛実賞 工芸の現在」(菊池寛実記念 智美術館/東京)
2016 「知命—50代の挑戦展」(伊丹市立工芸センター/兵庫)
2017 「所蔵作品展 動物集合」(東京国立近代美術館工芸館)
「漆芸〜伝統と革新の美〜」(三島大社宝物館/静岡)
「平成の至實 八十三選展」(薬師寺/奈良)
2018 「漆の現在2018展」(日本橋三越本店/東京)
「URUSHI 伝統と革新展」(石川県立美術館ほか)
「ジャポニズム150年展」(パリ装飾美術館/フランス)
2019 「現代工芸の展開展」(金沢市立安江金箔工芸館/石川)['22]
2020 「明治の工芸/平成の工芸—150年の時代を超えた日本のわざと装飾の美展」(現代ギリシャ文化博物館/ギリシャ)
2021 「漆の系譜展」(東北芸術工科大学/山形)
「文化を継承する埼玉の工芸作家 人間国宝の茶道具を中心に」(入間市博物館/埼玉)

主な受賞歴

1989 「第6回日本伝統漆芸展」文化庁長官賞
1993 「第40回日本伝統工芸展」日本工芸会奨励賞
1996 「第43回日本伝統工芸展」東京都知事賞
1997 「第44回日本伝統工芸展」日本工芸会奨励賞
2000 「第8回漆の美展」日本漆工協会会長賞
2002 第13回MOA岡田茂吉賞 工芸部門優秀賞
2002 「第10回漆の美展」文部科学大臣奨励賞
2008 「第16回漆の美展」農林水産省大臣賞
2018 「第25回漆の美展」文部科学大臣賞
2023 「第30回漆の美展」農林水産大臣賞

展覧会図録

- 『日蘭交流400周年記念日本現代漆芸展』、ヤン・ファン・デルトフト美術館、2000年
- 『Contemporary Japanese crafts: materials and way of formative thinking』、ペトロナス・ギャラリー・インドネシア国立美術館、2002年
- 『第13回MOA岡田茂吉賞展』、MOA美術館、2002年［第19回：2014年］
- 『わざの美　日本伝統工芸展50年記念展』、日本橋三越本店・山口美術館、2003年
- 『六葉會　18人の工芸家たち』、日本橋三越本店本館6階美術特選画廊、2004年
- 『工芸の力―21世紀の展望』、東京国立近代美術館、2007年
- 『手のひらの宇宙』（新霽シリーズ7）、ギャラリー竹柳堂、2008年
- 『光～歌会始御題によせて　平成の御題を振り返る　天皇陛下御即位三十年神宮美術館開館二十五周年記念特別展』、式年遷宮記念神宮美術館、2010年
- 『日本伝統工芸展60回記念　工芸からKŌGEIへ展』、東京国立近代美術館、2013年
- 『Beauty of Kōgei: art crafts in Japan』、国際交流基金アジアセンター、2014年
- 『菊池寛実賞　工芸の現在』、菊池寛実記念 智美術館、2015年
- 『平成の至寶　八十三選展』、薬師寺、2017年
- 『漆の現在2018展』、日本橋三越本店、2018年
- 『工藝2020―自然と美のかたち―』、東京国立博物館、2020年
- 『第40回日本伝統漆芸展』、西武池袋本店ほか、2023年

書籍

- 九つの音色刊行委員会『九つの音色　父の背を見て』、里文出版、2001年
- 『九つの音色―再美日本』刊行委員会『九つの音色　再美日本』、里文出版、2003年
- 九つの音色刊行委員会『九つの音色　藝術の対話　中国　韓国　そして日本』、里文出版、2005年
- 九つの音色刊行委員会『九つの音色　つたえあい』、里文出版、2007年
- 九つの音色刊行委員会『九つの音色　祈りの継承』、里文出版、2009年
- 『コロナ禍で楽しむ手工芸「誌上作品展」写真集』、日本手工芸作家連合会、2020年
- 『工芸会×飛鳥クルーズ　オフィシャルガイドブック』、2022年

定期刊行物

- 田口義明「海を渡った日本漆器III（技法と表現）」、『日本の美術』No.428、至文堂、2002年
- 田口義明「「工芸の力：21世紀の展望」展によせて」、『現代の眼』No.567、東京国立近代美術館、2007年12月号
- 田口義明「名匠の肖像　親子で取り組んだ修復 田口義明」、『週刊人間国宝』（週刊朝日百科）、朝日新聞社、No.54、2007年6月号

WEB

- 『田口義明　漆　蒔絵　螺鈿』（http://www.makie-yoshiaki.com/）［2022年12月27日最終アクセス］

田中信行 | Tanaka Nobuyuki

1959 東京都生まれ
1985 東京芸術大学大学院美術研究科漆芸専攻修了
1999 金沢美術工芸大学工芸科准教授、現在教授（2008–）

1959 Born in Tokyo
1985 Completes graduate studies in *Urushi*-Art (Japanese Lacquer), Tokyo University of the Arts
1999 Becomes Associate Professor, Department of Crafts, Kanazawa College of Art (Full Professor since 2008)

主な個展

1989 個展（ギャラリー山口／東京）['90, '96]
1992 個展（ときわ画廊／東京）
1993 個展（モリスギャラリー／東京）
1994 個展（マスダスタジオ／東京）
1996 個展（ギャルリ・プス／東京）
1998 「「工芸的なるもの」をめぐって（北澤憲昭連続企画Vol.1）」（ギャラリーマキ／東京）
1999 個展（エキジビション・スペース／東京）
2004 「NOBUYUKI TANAKA　Japanese Lacquer：Urushi」（KOICHI YANAGI Oriental Fine Art／ニューヨーク）['08, '11, '15]
2009 「漆が喚起するもの」（入善町 下山芸術の森 発電所美術館／富山）
2010 「The Tactile Memory」（日本橋髙島屋本店美術画廊X／東京）
2014 「田中信行新作展」（ケンジタキギャラリー／東京）['17]
2016 「Imaginary Skin」（上野の森美術館ギャラリー／東京・金沢アートグミ／石川）['17]
2017 「田中信行の茶室—流れる水　ふれる水」（山口県立萩美術館・浦上記念館／山口）
2018 「NOBUYUKI TANAKA—Urformen Primordial Memories—：田中信行 原形—原初の記憶—」（カイザースラウテルン美術館・ミュンスター漆美術館／ドイツ）['19]

主なグループ展

1987 「—WORKS—漆・空間への対応展」（ワコール銀座アートスペース／東京）
1988 「LACQUER ART & CRAFT展」（渋谷西武工芸画廊／東京）['91]
1989 「三木茂夫追悼展」（東京芸術大学展示室）
1991 「現代彫刻展—12人の新鋭作家達—」（KSPギャラリー／神奈川）
「加藤寿彦・田中信行二人展」（ギャラリー古川／東京）
1992 「日中現代漆芸展」（中国福建省）
1993 「塗りの系譜展」（東京国立近代美術館工芸館）
「ジャパンデザインコンペティション石川」（石川県産業展示館）
1994 「素材の領分展」（東京国立近代美術館工芸館）
「アジアの心とかたち—物質と創造力—展」（NTTクレドホール／広島）
「漆の現在性展」（神奈川県民ホールギャラリー）
「嗜欲の器展」（ギャラリーいそがや／東京）
「現代漆作家展」（スタジオコム／京都）
1995 「地の力展」（東京藝術大学大学美術館取手館／茨城）
「現代美術の展望　VOCA展'95」（上野の森美術館／東京）
「現代作家立体小品展」（ギャラリーマロニエ／京都ほか）['96, '97]
1996 「世界の漆、うるし展」（フジタヴァンテミュージアム／東京）
「生まれてくる者へのメッセージ展」（スペースかたち／東京）
「第1回日韓現代漆交流展」（ロッテアートギャラリー／韓国ほか）['98, '00]
「虹色の光彩　現代日本漆芸展」（ジャパン・ソサエティ・ギャラリー／ニューヨークほか）
「第2回美の予感展」（日本橋髙島屋／東京ほか）
1998 「Nature as object」（西オーストラリア州立美術館）
2000 「オブジェと置物—工芸と彫刻のあいだ展」（高岡市美術館／富山）
「日蘭交流400周年記念日本現代漆芸展」（ヤン・ファン・デル・トフト美術館／アムステルダムほか）
「The International Asian Art Fair」（ニューヨーク）
2001 「Life／art'01」（資生堂ギャラリー／東京）['02–'05]
2002 「伝統と革新　やきものとうるし展」（広島県立美術館）
2003 「テクスチャーとその意味—美大の非日常展」（金沢美術工芸大学／石川）
「工芸群像展I—気鋭の七人が形どる—展」（髙島屋日本橋本店／東京ほか）
2004 「前進する工芸展」（広島市市民交流プラザギャラリーほか）
「工芸群像展II—気鋭の七人が形どる—展」（髙島屋横浜店／神奈川ほか）
「机上空間のためのオブジェX展」（コンテンポラリーアートNIKI／東京）
2005 「アルス・ノーヴァー現代美術と工芸のはざまに」（東京都現代美術館）
2006 「Japan & Korea 漆 arts　exhibition展」（東京藝術大学美術館ほか）
2007 「六本木クロッシング2007　未来への脈動展」（森美術館／東京）
「清州国際工芸ビエンナーレ2007　Crafts: A Mode of Life展」（清州／韓国）
「宇宙御絵図」（豊田市美術館／愛知）
2008 「JAPAN! CULTURE + HYPER　CULTURE」（ジョン・F・ケネディ・センター／ワシントンD.C.）
2010 「漆のチカラ：漆文化の歴史と漆表現の現在展」（福島県立美術館）
「湖北国際漆トリエンナーレ」（湖北省美術館／武漢）['13, '16, '19, '23]
「第1回金沢世界工芸トリエンナーレ」（金沢21世紀美術館／石川）

2011 「漆展—新しい漆のかたち—展」(伊丹市立工芸センター/兵庫)
「サイレント・エコーI展」(金沢21世紀美術館/石川)
「美へ挑む 漆の輝き—近現代日本の漆芸展」(浦添市美術館/沖縄)
2012 「会津・漆の芸術祭」(会津若松山市・喜多方市/福島)
「現代造形のゆくえ—素材は語る—展」(樂翠亭美術館/富山)
「現代の座標—工芸をめぐる11の思考—」(東京国立近代美術館工芸館)
2013 「黒田辰秋・田中信行—漆という力—」(豊田市美術館/愛知)
2015 「シンプルなかたち」(森美術館/東京ほか)
2016 「革新の工芸"伝統と前衛"、そして現代」(東京国立近代美術館工芸館)
2017 「奥能登国際芸術祭2017」(珠洲市/石川)['21]
髙島屋美術部創設110年記念展「原初の思考」(髙島屋日本橋本店/東京ほか)
「Hard Bodies: Contemporary Japanese Lacquer Sculpture」(ミネアポリス美術館/アメリカ)
2019 「アジアのイメージ—日本美術の東洋憧憬—」(東京都庭園美術館)
開館15周年記念「現在地—未来の地図を描くために」(金沢21世紀美術館/石川)
2021 「北陸工芸の祭典 GO FOR KOGEI 2021(那谷寺/石川ほか)
「第1回蘇州工芸ビエンナーレ」(蘇州高新区馬山会議センター/中国)
2022 「Finale—Director's Cut」(カイザースラウテン美術館/ドイツ)
「サンセット/サンライズ」(豊田市美術館/愛知)
「色・形・モチーフ」(広島県立美術館)

主な受賞歴

1987 「第5回朝日現代クラフト展」奨励賞
1989 ジャパンデザインコンペティション石川 銀賞
2003 第14回タカシマヤ文化基金タカシマヤ美術賞
2012 第18回MOA岡田茂吉賞工芸部門大賞
2021 「第1回蘇州工芸ビエンナーレ」(中国)優秀賞

展覧会図録

- 『塗りの系譜』、東京国立近代美術館、1993年
- 『素材の領分』、東京国立近代美術館、1994年
- 『現代美術の展望 VOCA展'95』、上野の森美術館、1995年
- 『Life/art'01』、資生堂ギャラリー、2001年
- 『NOBUYUKI TANAKA Japanese Lacquer: Urushi』、KOICHI YANAGI Oriental Fine Art、2004年
- 『六本木クロッシング2007 未来への脈動』、森美術館、2007年
- 『漆が喚起するもの』、入善町 下山芸術の森 発電所美術館、2009年
- 『現代の座標 工芸をめぐる11の思考』、東京国立近代美術館、2012年
- 『黒田辰秋・田中信行—漆という力—』、豊田市美術館、2013年
- 『シンプルなかたち展』、森美術館、2015年
- 『革新の工芸—"伝統と前衛"、そして現代—』、東京国立近代美術館、2016年
- 『奥能登国際芸術祭 2017』、奥能登国際芸術祭実行委員会、2018年
- 『奥能登国際芸術祭 公式ガイドブック 2020+』、奥能登国際芸術祭実行委員会、2021年
- 『Hard Bodies: Contemporary Japanese Lacquer Sculpture』、ミネアポリス美術館、2017年
- 『NOBUYUKI TANAKA—Urformen Primordial Memories—』、カイザースラウテルン美術館・ミュンスター漆美術館、2018年
- 『アジアのイメージ—日本美術の東洋憧憬—』、東京都庭園美術館、2019年

書籍

- 北澤憲昭『アヴァンギャルドの以後の工芸 「工芸的なるもの」をもとめて』、美学出版、2003年
- 中村英樹『視覚の断層 開かれた自己生成のために』、現代企画室、2003年
- 「工芸」シンポジウム記録集編集委員会編『美術史の余白に 工芸・アルス・現代美術』、美学出版、2008年

定期刊行物

- 不動美里「田中信行—漆が喚起するもの」、『REAR』No.23、リア制作室、2010年3月号
- 天野一夫『月刊美術』No.486、株式会社サン・アート、2016年3月号
- 森孝一「思考の経路」、『アートコレクターズ』No.160、生活の友社、2022年7月号

坪島悠貴 | Tsuboshima Yuki

1987 東京都生まれ
2013 武蔵野美術大学大学院修士課程工芸工業デザインコース修了

1987 Born in Tokyo
2013 Completes master's course in Industrial, Interior, and Craft Design at Musashino Art University

主な個展

2012 「INSIDE 坪島悠貴展」(ギャラリー銀座フォレスト/東京)
2015 「Transformation」(Space2*3/東京)
「Double Meaning」(NANATASU GALLERY/東京)
2018 「可変金物—変形する金工作品」(三省堂書店池袋本店/東京)

主なグループ展

2013 「in alternative 武蔵野美術大学大学院工芸工業デザインコース修了制作展」(ギャラリーLE DECO/東京)
「ART Meeting展」(銀座三越/東京)
「EMERGING DIRECTORS'ARTFAIR ULTRA006」(青山スパイラルガーデン MITSUI ARTブース/東京)
「UMARTs2013 うまからうまれる15のアート」(馬の博物館/神奈川)
「ARTISTS'CAFÉ 7」展(銀座モダンアート/東京)
2014 「Space2*3取り扱い作家小品展」(Space2*3/東京)['15]
「SICF 15」(青山スパイラルガーデン/東京)
「金属工芸作家による根付展」(Gallery花影抄/東京)['16]
「KANAYA ONSHITSU MUSEUM」(Gallery工房 親/千葉)
「THE ARTFAIR+PLUS-ULTRA2014」(青山スパイラルガーデン/東京)['15]
2016 「3人のたなごころ展」(日本橋三越本店本館6階アートスクエア/東京)
2018 「Art Expo Malaysia Plus 2018」(MATRADE Exhibition and Convention Centre Gallery花影抄ブース/クアラルンプール)
「金工作家による根付と置物展」(日本橋三越本店本館6階美術工芸サロン/東京)['20, '22]
2021 「思考×機構×技巧 上原万征・坪島悠貴 二人展」(Gallery花影抄/東京)

主な受賞歴

2011 「第50回記念北陸中日美術展」工芸賞
2013 「平成24年度武蔵野美術大学卒業・修了制作展」優秀賞

書籍

- オートデスク株式会社編『Fusion 360 Masters』、ソーテック社、2017年

定期刊行物

- 「気鋭作家60人の"たなごころの美"」『月刊美術』No.459、サン・アート、2013年12月号
- 「2015年を大予測! 完売作家全データ」『月刊アートコレクターズ』No.58、生活の友社、2014年1月号
- 「展覧会レポート」『月刊アートコレクターズ』No.73、生活の友社、2015年4月号
- 「展覧会レビュー」『月刊美術』No.476、サン・アート、2015年5月号
- 「世界を「アッ」と言わせる、手わざとカタチ!!「超・立体」アートとしての最新工芸」『月刊美術』No.457、サン・アート、2017年2月号
- 「「用の美」×超・工芸EXTRA」『月刊美術』No.513、サン・アート、2018年6月号
- 「『装う』アートの最新形(ニューモード)」『月刊美術』No. 537、サン・アート、2020年6月号
- 『monoマガジン』No.873、マガジンハウス、2021年6月16日号
- 「特集 現代根付」『JJDA』No.56、公益社団法人日本ジュエリーデザイナー協会、2022年

WEB

- 『坪島悠貴—可変金物、彫金、金工—Wix.com』(https://tsuboyuki79.wixsite.com/website)[2022年12月27日最終アクセス]
- 「金属造型作家 坪島悠貴さんのご紹介」『キャド研』(https://cad-kenkyujo.com/3763/)[2022年12月27日最終アクセス]
- 「坪島悠貴/金属造形作家」『Get Wel』(https://www.youtube.com/watch?v=ELYZ1I-MY8U&t=1s)[2022年12月27日最終アクセス]
- 「フグから鳳凰にトランスフォーム! カチッとハマるギミックに惚れぼれする」『おたくま経済新聞』(https://otakei.otakuma.net/archives/2019041803.html)[2022年12月28日最終アクセス]
- 「3Dプリンタの明日を妄想する 第22回 金属造形作家が3Dプリンタに出会って」『3D CREATERS.JP』(http://3dcreators.jp/column/ms_22.shtml)[2022年12月23日最終アクセス]
- 「可変福獣骨」『これやん』(https://koreyan.jp/yukitsuboshima/3684/)[2022年12月23日最終アクセス]
- 「金属のセミがカエルに変形! 造形作家の職人技「可変角蛙」」『KAI-YOU』(https://kai-you.net/article/78478)[2022年12月27日最終アクセス]
- 「創造人×話 坪島悠貴さんインタビュー」『岩崎電気株式会社』(https://www.iwasaki.co.jp/corporate/talk/26_tsuboshima-02.html)[2022年12月27日最終アクセス]
- 「エデのその後」『武蔵野美術大学 工芸工業デザイン学科』(https://koude.musabi.ac.jp/interviews/198/)[2022年12月27日最終アクセス]
- 「アートか、ホビーか? 変形する金属彫刻を作りつづける造形作家、坪島悠貴の幻想世界【ホビー業界インサイド第81回】」『アキバ総研』(https://akiba-souken.com/article/56493/)[2022年12月27日最終アクセス]
- 「クリエイターFILE#13 可変金属模型」『nextクリエイターズ(日本テレビ)』(https://www.ntv.co.jp/nextcreators/backnumber/creator13.html)[2022年12月27日最終アクセス]
- 「225 坪島悠貴[金属造形作家]」『デザインコード(テレビ朝日)』[2022年12月27日最終アクセス]

新實広記｜Niimi Hiroki

1976 愛知県生まれ
2001 愛知教育大学大学院教育学研究科芸術教育専攻修士課程修了
「CGCA（creative glass center of America）fellowship」招待作家（ウィートンビレッジ／ニュージャージー州）
2015 「Vessel」設置（大手門タワーJXビル／東京）
2019 「Vessel」設置（PARK FRONT 香椎照葉／福岡）
2020 「Vessel」設置（Hotel olein／静岡）

1976 Born in Aichi Prefecture
2001 Completes Master of Arts in Education Program at Graduate School of Education, Aichi University of Education
Invited artist fellowship at Creative Glass Center of America (CGCA) (Wheaton Village, New Jersey)
2015 "Vessel" installation (Ōtemon Tower JX Building, Tokyo)
2019 "Vessel" installation (Park Front Kashii-teriha, Fukuoka)
2020 "Vessel" installation (Hotel Olein, Shizuoka)

主な個展

2007 「再生による構築」（ギャラリープラネット／愛知）
2011 「農村舞台アートプロジェクト」（細田神社農村舞台／愛知）［加塩神社農村舞台：'14］
2013 「Vessels」（Masayoshi Suzuki Gallery／愛知）
2017 「新實広記展—名づけられた光（Cassina ixc. DELL'ARTE Art Gallery／青山）
2018 「光の図形」（Masayoshi Suzuki Gallery／愛知）
「VESSEL—光のうつわ—」（豊田市民芸の森 旧本多静雄亭／愛知）

主なグループ展

2002 「豊田の彫刻家たち」（豊田市美術館市民ギャラリー／愛知）
2003 「20/20 VISION」（ミュージアム・オブ・アメリカン・グラス／ニュージャージー）
「GLASS WEEKEND」（ウィートンビレッジ／ニュージャージー）
「とよたの新世代」（豊田市美術館市民ギャラリー／愛知）
2005 「GLASS ART NOW 東海の現代ガラス展」（瀬戸市新世紀工芸館／愛知）
2008 「喜楽亭—10の響—」（豊田産業文化センター／愛知）
2009 「FLAT GLASS—平面から浮かぶもの—」（瀬戸市新世紀工芸館／愛知）
「ガラスの変貌」（ギャラリーヴォイス／岐阜）
2011 「瀬戸市新世紀工芸館企画 新實広記・畑中篤 二人展」（瀬戸市新世紀工芸館／愛知）
「SELECTION：01」（Masayoshi Suzuki Gallery／愛知）
2012 「ARTIST FILE 04」（Masayoshi Suzuki Gallery／愛知）
2016 「feeling glass 感じとるかたち」（富山市ガラス美術館）
「とよたルミアール・プロジェクト」（豊田市役所東庁舎／愛知）
「現代ガラスの表現展」（大一美術館／名古屋）
2018 「第7回現代ガラス展in山陽小野田」（おのだサンパーク／山口）
2022 「国際ガラス年 2022 ガラス展 E-to-ten」（東京大学安田講堂）
「After Prize—豊田の美術」（豊田市美術館ギャラリー／愛知）

主な受賞歴

2018 「第7回現代ガラス展in山陽小野田」土屋審査員賞

展覧会図録

- 『feeling in glass 感じとるかたち』、富山市ガラス美術館、2016年
- 「若き創造者たちの「宇宙」」『第7回現代ガラス展 in 山陽小野田』、現代ガラス展実行委員会、2018年
- 『新實広記展—名づけられた光』、Cassina ixc. DELL'ARTE Art Gallery、2017年

書籍

- 『ガラス工芸家100人 現代日本の精鋭たち』（別冊炎芸術）、阿部出版、2021年
- 『25 Years of New Glass Review』、The Corning Museum of Glass、2005年
- 『日本の現代ガラス作家』、旭硝子、2003年

WEB

- 「ガラス作家 新實広記—インタビュー」『カッシーナ・イクスシー』（https://www.cassina-ixc.jp/shop/t/t1626/）［2023年1月4日最終アクセス］

その他

- 大手門タワー・JXビルパンフレット、三菱地所、JXホールディングス
- 「パークフロント香椎照葉」『PARK FRONTE ART BOOK』、積水ハウス株式会社、西日本鉄道株式会社、西部ガスリビング株式会社

林茂樹 | Hayashi Shigeki

1972 岐阜県生まれ
1995 静岡県立大学国際関係学部国際関係学科卒業
1997 岐阜県立多治見工業高等学校陶磁科学芸術専攻科修了

1972 Born in Gifu Prefecture
1995 Graduates from School of International Relations, University of Shizuoka
1997 Completes studies in ceramics at Gifu Prefectural Tajimi Technical High School

主な個展

2004 「Entertainment Ceramics」(スペース大原/岐阜)['06, '12, '16, '20]
2006 「New type Ceramics」(夢創館/兵庫)['08]
2011 「Breakthrough Ceramics」(松坂屋名古屋店/愛知)
「Accelerated Ceramics」(新宿髙島屋、日本橋髙島屋/東京)
2012 「mOOn Rider」(阿久津画廊/群馬)
2016 「Unfolded Ceramics」(日本橋髙島屋/東京ほか)
2022 「DISCOVER CERAMICS」(日本橋髙島屋/東京ほか)

主なグループ展

2004 「MINO CERAMICS NOW」(岐阜県現代陶芸美術館)['12]
2008 「Artistic Christmas」(新宿髙島屋/東京)[–'15]
2010 「アート台北」(台北世界貿易中心)[–'12]
「アートフェア東京」(東京国際フォーラム)['11, '13, '14, '16]
2011 「Art HK」(Hong Kong Convention and Exhibition Centre/香港)
2012 「ヴァロリス国際陶芸展」(ヴァロリス陶芸美術館/フランス)
「Ceramic/Figurative」(日本橋髙島屋、新宿髙島屋/東京)
2013 「第8回パラミタ陶芸大賞展」(パラミタミュージアム/三重)
「COLLECT」(Saatchi Gallery/ロンドン)[–'15]
2014 「やきものって何ダ?―陶芸美術館8館の名品に学ぶ―」(兵庫陶芸美術館ほか)
「Art Stage Singapore」(Marina Bay Sands/シンガポール)[–'16]
「Art Miami」(One Herald Plaza/アメリカ)['15, '19]
2015 「TOKYO DESIGN WEEK in MILANO」(Padiglione Visconti/ミラノ)
「Contemporary Art in RAKUSUITEI」(樂翠亭美術館/富山)
2016 「BIWAKOビエンナーレ2016」(近江八幡旧市街/滋賀)
2017 「新宿髙島屋10周年記念～そして広がる～」(新宿髙島屋/東京)
2018 「Four Rooms+1 4つの和室と蔵にみる現代美術」(樂翠亭美術館/富山)
「風詠抄―譚」(日本橋髙島屋/東京)
2019 「第25回日本陶芸展」(大丸東京ほか)
「驚異!! セラミック・スカルプチャー～奇々怪々な異形たち」(Bunkamura Gallery/東京)
「土複合の彫刻家たち展」(現代彫刻美術館/東京)
「鋳込み・IKOMI・2019」(とうしん美濃陶芸美術館/岐阜)
2020 「Metropolis 2020」(日本橋髙島屋/東京)
「ブレイク前夜 小山登美夫セレクションのアーティスト38人」(代官山ヒルサイドテラス/東京)
2021 「No Man's Land―陶芸の未来、未だ見ぬ地平の先―」(兵庫陶芸美術館)
「素材転生 Beyond the Material」(岐阜県美術館)
2022 「Trans⇔Form―変容シテユクカタチ」(日本橋髙島屋/東京)
2023 「TOKYO☆Neo Duo Exhibition」(Japan Creative Center/シンガポール)

主な受賞歴

1999 「第2回ユーモア陶彫展'99」審査員特別賞
2004 「第9回日本現代陶彫展」陶彫展賞
2007 「55回ファエンツァ国際陶芸展」下院議長賞
2008 「第8回国際陶磁器展」銅賞・美濃賞
「たけしの誰でもピカソ 激突! アートバトル2008」チャンピオン
2011 「57回ファエンツァ国際陶芸展」大賞

展覧会図録

- 『第2回ユーモア陶彫展'99』、セラトピア土岐、1999年
- 『第9回日本現代陶彫展 2004』、セラテクノ土岐、2004年
- 『MINO CERAMICS NOW 2004「美濃」から「MINO」へ―世界へ発信する伝統と現代の陶芸家たち』、岐阜県現代陶芸美術館、2004年
- 『美濃陶磁展:国際陶磁器フェスティバル美濃'05協賛』、多治見市産業文化センター、2005年
- 『日本×ファエンツァやきものの現在 ファエンツァ国際陶芸展日本人歴代受賞作家展』、イタリア文化会館・多治見市文化工房ギャラリーヴォイス、2011年
- 『MINO CERAMICS NOW 2012―MINO陶芸の気鋭―』、岐阜県現代陶芸美術館、2012年
- 『素材転生―Beyond the Material』、岐阜県美術館、2021年
- 『No Man's Land―陶芸の未来、未だ見ぬ地平の先―』、兵庫陶芸美術館、2021年

書籍

- 『現代日本の陶芸 vol.3』、ART BOXインターナショナル、2011年
- 『現代美術アーティストファイルIV』、ART BOXインターナショナル、2015年
- 『陶芸家150人 2020年現代日本の精鋭たち』(別冊炎芸術)、阿部出版、2020年

定期刊行物

- 「イケテル陶芸 熱くてクールな、未来の千両役者たち」『月刊美術』No.431、サン・アート、2011年8月号
- 「期待の新人 林茂樹、和田山真央」『炎芸術』No.115、阿部出版、2013年8月号
- 「注目の立体作家106人!」『月刊アートコレクターズ』No.58 、生活の友社、2014年1月号
- 「超・工芸の最前線」『月刊美術』No.486、サン・アート、2016年3月号
- 「今、注目の陶芸家30人」『炎芸術』No.129、阿部出版、2017年2月号
- 「陶の人形 命のかたち」『炎芸術』No.132、阿部出版、2017年11月号
- 「新・現代陶芸入門」『炎芸術』No.143、阿部出版、2020年8月号
- 「百貨店×現代アートの最前線」『月刊美術』No.566、2022年11月号

WEB

- 「教職員紹介 林茂樹」『多摩美術大学 工芸学科』(https://www.tamabi.ac.jp/kougei/ceramic/staff_hayashi_shigeki.html)[2022年12月27日最終アクセス]

葉山有樹 | Hayama Yuki

1961　佐賀県生まれ
1975　佐賀県立有田工業高等学校デザイン科(夜学)入学
佐賀県有田町の窯元に入社、陶磁器製作を8年間学ぶ
1985　佐賀県武雄市山内町にて「葉山窯」開窯
工房移転、長男の名を雅号に取り現在の「葉山有樹窯」とする
2005　『詩想の旋律　葉山有樹作品集』(新日本教育図書)を出版
2007　イッタラ社アラビア窯アートデパートメント(フィンランド)にて滞在制作(–2008)

1961 Born in Saga Prefecture
1975 Enters Design Department, Saga Prefectural Arita Technical High School (night school)
Joins kiln in Arita, Saga Prefecture, and studies ceramics-making for eight years
1985 Opens Hayama Kiln in Yamauchi, Takeo City, Saga Prefecture
Relocates and founds Hayama Yuki Kiln, named for eldest son
2005 Book *The Melody of Poetic Imagination: the Yuki Hayama Collection* published by Shin-Nippon Kyoiku Tosho Co., Ltd.
2007 Artist in residence at the Art Department Society, Iittala & Arabia Design Centre (Finland) (until 2008)

主な個展

1990　個展(博多全日空ホテル／博多)
1991　「細密画の世界展」(東京アメリカンクラブ)
1998　「葉山有樹展」(O・A・Gドイツ文化会館／赤坂)
2007　「A Pattern Odyssey 葉山有樹展」(青山スパイラルガーデン／東京)
「Ceramics story YUKI HAYAMA EXHIBITION」(フィンランド・デザインミュージアム／ヘルシンキ)['08]
2008　「魚になった少女」出版記念展(青山スパイラルガーデン／東京)
2016　「YUKI HAYAMA EXHIBITION BEAUTY OF LIFE：葉山有樹展　生命の美」(Joseph Carini Carpets／ニューヨーク)
2021　「THE GARDEN OF DREAMS：千年の華」(Ippodo Gallery／ニューヨーク)
「Yuki Hayama」(Pierre Marie Giraud／ブリュッセル)
2022　「虹の彼方に」(飯高寺／千葉)

主なグループ展

1991　グループ展(ウラクメインギャラリー／東京)
2008　「Neo Japonisme—日仏友好150周年記念展—」(横浜山手西洋館／神奈川)
「2008年山手西洋館フェスタJUNE〜花と器のハーモニー〜」(横浜山手西洋館／神奈川)
2010　「空飛ぶだんごむし」出版記念展(青山スパイラルガーデン／東京)
2011　「KAITEKIのかたち〜アートと技術の科学反応〜展」(青山スパイラルガーデン／東京)
2012　「工芸未来派」(金沢21世紀美術館／石川)
2014　「道後オンセナート2014」(HOTEL HORIZONTAL：道後温泉ふなや／愛媛)
2015　「Japanese Kogei Future Forward」(The Museum of Arts and Design／ニューヨーク)
2018　「三人展—明日への眼差し—」(佐賀県立美術館)

展覧会図録

- 『葉山有樹作品集　A pattern odyssey 文様をめぐる450万年の旅』、青山スパイラルガーデン、2007年
- 『工芸未来派』、金沢21世紀美術館、2012年
- 『葉山有樹展　生命の美』、Ippodo Gallery、2016年
- 『無常　葉山有樹作品集』、佐賀県立美術館、2018年

書籍

- 葉山有樹『千年の華—細密画の世界—葉山有樹作品集』、葉山有樹窯、2002年
- 葉山有樹『詩想の旋律　葉山有樹作品集』、新日本教育図書、2005年
- 葉山有樹『文様の変遷　葉山有樹展』、葉山有樹窯、2007年
- 葉山有樹『神話の波紋—玻璃と剣—』、風濤社、2008年
- 葉山有樹『魚になった少女』、風濤社、2008年
- 葉山有樹『空飛ぶだんごむし』、風濤社、2010年
- 木村俊介『仕事の話　日本のスペシャリスト32人が語る「やり直し、繰り返し」』、文藝春秋、2011年
- 葉山有樹『種子集』、ブイツーソリューション、2012年
- 秋元雄史『工芸未来派　アート化する新しい工芸』、六耀社、2016年

福田亨｜Fukuda Toru

1994 北海道生まれ
2013 北海道おといねっぷ美術工芸高等学校工芸科卒業
2015 京都伝統工芸大学校木工芸専攻卒業

1994 Born in Hokkaido
2013 Graduates from crafts department, Hokkaido Otoineppu Arts and Crafts High School
2015 Graduates from Traditional Arts Super College of Kyoto, majoring in woodcrafts

主な個展

2019 「福田亨展」(靖山画廊／東京)
2021 「福田亨—Mushikago—」(SEIZAN GALLERY TOKYO 凸／東京)
「TORU FUKUDA ni-wa」(靖山画廊／東京)

主なグループ展

2017 「現代日本の匠」(Hideharu Fukasaku Gallery Roppongi／東京)
「Spring ephemeral」(Atelier cypris／大阪)
「たいせつなもの展」(靖山画廊／東京)[-'19]
2018 「木霊する場所—木の造形展—」(悠遊舎ぎゃらりぃ／愛知)
2019 「木のものづくり探訪—20人の仕事—」(リビングデザインセンターOZONE／東京)
「蟲使い展」(f.e.i art gallery／神奈川)
「INSECTS」(ギャラリーアートもりもと／東京)['21, '22]
「mima-no-me #みまのめ〈VOL. 5〉」(北海道立三岸好太郎美術館)
「KOGEI Art Fair Kanazawa 2019」悠遊舎ぎゃらりぃSAPPOROスペース(KUMU金沢／石川)
2020 「鱗翅目三人展」(Atelier cypris／大阪)
「LOOK CLOSER」(Micheko Galerie／ミュンヘン)
「PURE POETRY」(SEIZAN gallery／ニューヨーク)
2021 「美の予感 2021—もののあはれ—」(日本橋髙島屋／東京ほか)
2023 「超絶技巧、未来へ! 明治工芸とそのDNA」(岐阜県現代陶芸美術館ほか)

展覧会図録

- 『もののあはれ』、高島屋日本橋店ほか、2021年

書籍

- 芸術新聞社監修『現代彫刻アンソロジー』、芸術新聞社、2020年
- 丸山宗利監修『昆虫のとんでもない世界』(別冊太陽　日本のこころ282)、平凡社、2020年

定期刊行物

- 『月刊アートコレクターズ』No.111 、生活の友社、2019年3月号
- 「新世代9作家が語る、「今なぜ、昆虫の作品なのか?」」『月刊美術』No.528、2019年9月号、サン・アート
- 「北海道おといねっぷ美術工芸高等学校—小さな村の大きな夢」『approach』No.231、竹中工務店広報部、2020年9月
- 『月刊アートコレクターズ』No.142 、生活の友社、2021年1月号
- 「「いきもの」造形最前線」『炎芸術』No.146、阿部出版、2021年5月号
- 「昆虫学者・丸山宗利が気になる作家たち「昆虫アートはすごい」×7」『月刊美術』No.550、2021年7月号、サン・アート

WEB

- 「福田亨」『靖山画廊』(https://art-japan.jp/artists/2129/)[2022年12月27日最終アクセス]

桝本佳子｜Masumoto Keiko

1982 兵庫県生まれ
2007 京都市立芸術大学大学院修士課程陶磁器専攻修了
2010 フィラデルフィア芸術大学（ペンシルベニア）ゲストアーティスト
2013 ヴィクトリア＆アルバート美術館（ロンドン）レジデンスプログラムアーティスト
2020 滋賀県陶芸の森ゲストアーティスト
現在、滋賀県信楽町にて制作活動

1982 Born in Hyogo
2007 Completes master's program in ceramics at Graduate School of Arts, Kyoto City University of Arts
2010 Guest artist at University of the Arts, Philadelphia, Pennsylvania
2013 Artist in residence program at the Victoria & Albert Museum, London
2020 Guest artist at the Shigaraki Ceramic Cultural Park
Currently living and working in Shigaraki, Shiga Prefecture

主な個展

2004「くらしのなかのやきもの」（京都芸大ギャラリー）
2006「SEGMENT」（京都芸大ギャラリー）
2008「桝本佳子展」（石田大成社ホール／京都）
2009「皿と壺」（太陽事務／京都）
2010「陶のパノラマ」（INAXガレリアセラミカ／東京）
「桝本佳子展」（Gallery Jin Projects／東京）［'12］
2011「第22回美術の中のかたち—手で見る造形　桝本佳子展「やきもの変化」」（兵庫県立美術館）
2012「motif/vessel」（ICN gallery／ロンドン）
2014「特別展　とびだす／うつわ「桝本佳子の世界」」（たつの市立龍野歴史文化資料館／兵庫）
2017 アートフェア東京2017「Masumoto EXPO」（東京国際フォーラム 村越画廊ブース）
2021「Blue Birds/Blue Ceramics」（ワコールスタディホール／京都）
2022「春夏秋冬」（千總ギャラリー／京都）
「OVER GROWN」（Candy Bar Gallery／京都）

主なグループ展

2004「京都市立芸術大学陶磁器専攻　陶７人展」（くらふとギャラリー集／京都）
「くらしのなかのやきもの展」（京都芸大ギャラリー）
2005「京都→ソウル展」（toppohouse／ソウル）
グループ展（ブンパカ／大阪）
「新世代の交感展」（愛知県陶磁資料館）
2006 グループ展（café moni／京都）
2007「陶４人展」（ギャラリー風紋舎／京都）
2011「新・陶・宣言」（豊田市美術館／愛知）
2012「パラミタ陶芸大賞展」（パラミタミュージアム／岐阜）
2014「美の予感 2014—Metamorphose—」（髙島屋京都店ほか）
2018「Ascending Art Annual #2 まつり、まつる」（青山スパイラルガーデン／東京・ワコールスタディホール／京都）
2019「あいちトリエンナーレ2019」（愛知芸術文化センターほか）
2020「Co-LAB #3 大井康弘×桝本佳子＝xImage」（ボーダレス・アートミュージアムNO-MA／滋賀）
2021 八戸市美術館開館記念展「ギフト、ギフト、」（八戸市美術館／青森）
2022「ロマンティック・プログレス」（岐阜現代陶芸美術館）

主な受賞歴

2005「京都市立芸術大学制作展」同窓会賞
2006「国民文化祭やまぐち陶芸展」文部科学大臣賞
2007「京都市立芸術大学大学院修了制作展」大学院市長賞
2008「東京ミッドダウンアワードアートコンペ」準グランプリ
2009「京展　彫刻部門」館長奨励賞
「トーキョーワンダーウォール　立体・インスタレーション部門」大賞
2013 兵庫芸術奨励賞
2018 秀明文化基金賞

展覧会図録

- 『装飾の力＝The power of decoration』、東京国立近代美術館、2009年
- 『Residencies Toshiba Japanese Ceramics Resident: Keiko Masumoto April–September 2013』（ハンドアウト）、ヴィクトリア＆アルバート博物館、2013年
- 『とびだす／うつわ—桝本佳子の世界—』、たつの市立龍野歴史文化資料館、2014年
- 『Metamorphose　美の予感 2014』、髙島屋京都店ほか、2014年
- 『あいちトリエンナーレ2019＝AICHI TRIENNALE 2019：情の時代』、愛知芸術文化センターほか、2019年
- 『八戸市美術館開館記念「ギフト、ギフト、」』、八戸市美術館、2021年
- 『Romantic progress』、岐阜県現代陶芸美術館、2022年

定期刊行物

- 「世界を「アッ」と言わせる、手わざとカタチ！！「超・立体」アートとしての最新工芸」『月刊美術』No.457、サン・アート、2017年2月号
- 小吹隆文「関西の陶芸展」『陶説』No.819、公益社団法人日本陶磁協会、2021年8月号

水橋さおり | Mizuhashi Saori

1976 神奈川県生まれ
1996 文化女子大学短期大学生活造形学科卒業
2000 大塚きもの・テキスタイル専門学校卒業
染色家・坂井教人に師事
2010 独立
2021 女子美術大学非常勤講師(–現在)
2022 日本工芸会正会員

1976 Born in Kanagawa Prefecture
1996 Graduates from Department of Living Art and Design, Bunka Women's Junior College
2000 Graduates from Otsuka Kimono and Textiles College
Apprenticeship under master textiles dyer Sakai Norihito
2010 Establishes own studio
2021 Adjunct instructor at Joshibi University of Art and Design (ongoing)
2022 Becomes full member of Japan Kogei Association

主なグループ展

2000 「あお展　東京都工芸染色協同組合 青年部作品展」(東京藝術劇場地下ギャラリー)[–'14]
「第16回シルク博物館　全国染織作品展」(シルク博物館／神奈川)['06, '08, '10, '12]
2001 「第39回東京手描友禅 染芸展」(東京都産業貿易センター浜松町本館3階)[–'22]
「神奈川県美術展」(神奈川県民ホールギャラリーほか)[–'07]
2010 「友禅染の小物たち」(雪之下画廊／神奈川)[–'19]
「第50回東日本伝統工芸展」(日本橋三越本店／東京)['12, '18–'22]
2014 「第61回日本伝統工芸展」(日本橋三越本店ほか)['20, '22]
2020 「白からはじめる染しごと～海の巻～」展(大塚文庫／東京)[輪の巻：'21、空の巻：'22(イチマス田源／東京)]
2021 「第55回日本伝統工芸展染織展」(日本橋三越本店ほか)
「第28回伝統工芸・神奈川会展」(横浜高島屋／神奈川)['22]
2022 「第2回日本を継ぐ　日本工芸会東日本支部U50有志展」(丸善日本橋店／東京)['23]

主な受賞歴

2002 「第40回東京手描友禅 染芸展」技術賞
2006 「第19回シルク博物館全国染織作品展」奨励賞
2008 「第46回東京手描友禅 染芸展」佳作
2009 「第47回東京手描友禅 染芸展」奨励賞
2012 「第22回シルク博物館全国染織作品展」シルク博物館大賞
2013 「第51回東京手描友禅 染芸展」染芸展賞(青年部)
2014 「第61回日本伝統工芸展」奨励賞
2016 「第54回東京手描友禅 染芸展」東京都商工会議所会頭賞
2017 「第55回東京手描友禅 染芸展」染芸展賞
2022 「第29回伝統工芸・神奈川会展」会長賞

定期刊行物

- 「第19回シルク博物館全国染織作品展特集号」『染織春秋』No.434、八宝堂、2006年11月号
- 『和の生活マガジン花Saku』No.552、PR現代、2011年2月号
- 「第22回シルク博物館全国染織作品展特集号」『染織春秋』No.470、八宝堂、2012年11月号
- 『婦人画報』No.1338、ハースト婦人画報社、2015年1月号
- 『Yangon Press』No.35、Yangon Press(ミャンマー)、2016年5月号
- 『Yangon Press』No.39、Yangon Press(ミャンマー)、2016年9月号

満田晴穂｜Mitsuta Haruo

1980 鳥取県生まれ
2008 東京藝術大学大学院美術研究科修士課程彫金研究室修了
自在置物作家・冨木宗行（好山派冨木家当主）に師事

1980 Born in Tottori Prefecture
2008 Completes master's program in metal carving at Graduate School of Fine Arts, Tokyo University of the Arts
Apprenticeship under Tomiki Muneyuki (Kozan school), master craftsman of *jizai okimono* (articulated metal art objects)

主な個展

2006 「満田晴穂展」（ギャラリールポリエ／東京）
2010 「JIZAI」（ラディウムーレントゲンヴェルケ／東京）［'13, '15, '17］
2016 「JIZAI」（日本橋三越本店／東京）［'10, '12, '14, '18, '20, '22］
2020 「「自在」満田晴穂 個展」（古美術鐘ヶ江／京都）
2022 「自在置物 満田晴穂 細密進化の旅」（平山郁夫美術館／広島）
2023 特別企画展「満田晴穂 JIZAI」（米子市美術館／鳥取）

主なグループ展

2003 「23_3+K」（東京藝術大学美術館）
2004 「24_3+K」（東京藝術大学美術館）
2006 「東京藝術大学卒業修了制作展」（東京都美術館）
「全日本 金・銀創作展」（GINZA TANAKA HALL／東京）
2007 「いきもの展」（渋谷東急本店／東京）
「第2回藝大アートプラザ大賞入賞作品展」（藝大アートプラザ／東京）
「010 STUDIO EXHIBITION」（010 Gallery & Studio／茨城）
2008 「東京藝術大学卒業修了制作展」（東京藝術大学美術館）
「市民のための美術コレクションケア展」（千葉市美術館）
2009 「メークリヒカイトII」（ラディウムーレントゲンヴェルケ／東京）
「第48回日本クラフト展」（丸ビルホール／東京）
2010 「巧術」（青山スパイラルガーデン／東京）
「手数系」（AKI GALLERY／台湾）
「ネオ・リアリズム」（Bunkamuraギャラリー／東京）
2011 「掌10」（ラディウムーレントゲンヴェルケ／東京）
「手練～巧術其之貳」（青山スパイラルガーデン／東京）
2012 「蠱惑～巧術其之参」（青山スパイラルガーデン／東京）
2013 「アート昆虫ワールド」（高崎市タワー美術館／群馬）
「六本木クロッシング2013展：アウト・オブ・ダウト―来たるべき風景のために」（森美術館／東京）
「韜晦～巧術其之肆」（青山スパイラルガーデン／東京）
「溶ける魚―つづきの現実」（京都精華大学ギャラリーフロール）
2014 「縹渺～巧術其之伍」（ギャラリー点／石川）
2015 「濫觴～巧術其之陸」（ギャラリー点／石川）
2016 「isotope II」（ラディウムーレントゲンヴェルケ／東京）
「半肆半」（青山スパイラルガーデン／東京）
「俊傑～巧術其之柒」（ギャラリー点／石川）
「―未踏への具象―ざ・てわざ」（日本橋三越本店／東京）
「蜘蛛の糸」（豊田市美術館／愛知）
「今様 IMAYŌ: JAPAN'S NEW TRADITIONISTS」（ハワイ大学ギャラリー・ホノルル美術館）
「融合する工芸―旅に出たヤドカリのはなし」（大阪高島屋）
2017 「今様―昔と今をつなぐ」（松濤美術館／東京）
「カオスモス5 一粒の砂に世界を見るように」（佐倉市立美術館／千葉）
「金工の深化」（和光ホール／東京）［'21］
「ニッポンの写実 そっくりの魔力」（北海道立函館美術館ほか）
「驚威の超絶技巧！―明治工芸から現代アートへ―」（三井記念美術館／東京ほか）
2018 「混蟲圖鑑」（ラディウムーレントゲンヴェルケ／東京）
「融合する工芸―見つけた伝統のアシタ―」（和光ホール／東京）
「新装開店特別展」（古美術鐘ヶ江／京都）
2019 第4回金沢・世界工芸トリエンナーレ企画展「越境する工芸」（金沢21世紀美術館／石川）
2022 「リアル（写実）のゆくえ 現代の作家たち 生きること、写すこと」（平塚市美術館／神奈川ほか）

主な受賞歴

2006 「全日本 金・銀創作展」開催委員会会長賞
2007 「第2回藝大アートプラザ大賞入賞作品展」大賞
2017 平成28年度日本文化藝術奨学金 第8回創造する伝統賞

展覧会図録

- 『六本木クロッシング2013 アウト・オブ・ダウト来たるべき風景のために』、森美術館、2013年
- 『旅に出たヤドカリのはなし』、大阪高島屋6階美術画廊、2016年
- 『今様 昔と今をつなぐ』、渋谷区立松濤美術館、2017年
- 『驚異の超絶技巧！明治工芸から現代アートへ』、三井記念美術館ほか、2017年
- 『カオスモス5 一粒の砂に世界を見るように』、佐倉市立美術館、2017年
- 『金工の深化』、和光ホール、2017年
- 『見つけた伝統のアシタ』、和光ホール、2018年
- 『越境する工芸』、金沢21世紀美術館、2019年
- 『リアル（写実）のゆくえ 現代の作家たち 生きること、写すこと』、平塚市美術館ほか、2022年
- 『自在置物 満田晴穂 細密進化の旅』、平山郁夫美術館、2022年

書籍

- 四代田辺竹雲斎『四代田辺竹雲斎：守破離』、美術出版社、2021年

定期刊行物

- 「クローズアップ① 現代によみがえる「自在置物」—満田晴穂、驚愕の超絶技巧」『月刊美術』No.459、サン・アート、2013年12月号
- 「2015年を大予測! 完売作家全データ」『月刊アートコレクターズ』No.73、生活の友社、2015年4月号
- 「インタビュー　満田晴穂　「JIZAI」が生みだす特異点」『月刊美術』No.497、サン・アート、2017年2月号
- 『炎芸術』、阿部美術、2018年8月号
- 「こんなにも虫を愛でる文化があることをロンドンの人たちにも伝えたい（アトリエから語る 画家・今年の抱負）」『月刊美術』No.521、サン・アート、2019年2月号
- 「対談　自在置物でみる、「昆虫はすごい」満田晴穂×丸山宗利」『月刊美術』No.528、2019年9月号、サン・アート
- 「満田晴穂×丸山宗利　自在置物でみる「身近な昆虫はすごい」」『月刊美術』No.540・542・550・563、サン・アート、2020年9・11・21年7・22年8月号
＊第1回「オオスズメバチ：くびれと触角が物語る、最先端の機能美」、第2回「エンマコオロギ：日本の「鳴く虫」代表 その秘密は翅の模様にあり」、最終回スペシャル、「誌上販売特集　ムシとアートの相似形（フラクタル）2.5」
- 「和光ホール　金工の深化 II」『チャイム銀座』No.427、K＆Dコーポレーション、2021年5月号
- 「「いきもの」造形最前線」『炎芸術』No.146、阿部出版、2021年5月号

WEB

- 『満田晴穂と自在置物標本箱』(http://m-haruo.com/)[2022年12月20日最終アクセス]
- 「東京交差点#115「自在置物」—自在置物作家・満田晴穂」『テレビ東京公式　TV TOKYO』(https://www.youtube.com/watch?v=NL5LSxhsQdc)[2022年12月27日最終アクセス]
- 「自在作家 満田晴穂 ブレイク前夜〜次世代の芸術家たち〜　#40　超絶技巧作家（Haruo Mitsuta）」『ブレイク前夜』(https://www.youtube.com/watch?v=eshu5cYOZaU)[2022年12月27日最終アクセス]
- 「【超困難】「メタルクワガタ」の作り方自在置物作家・満田晴穂　How to make the metal stag beetle」『情熱大陸　公式チャンネル』(https://www.youtube.com/watch?v=Jfa9jJM3npA)[2022年12月27日最終アクセス]

吉田泰一郎 | Yoshida Taiichiro

1989 東京都生まれ
2013 東京藝術大学大学院美術研究科工芸専攻彫金修了
2014 東京藝術大学美術学部工芸科彫金教育研究助手(–2017)

1989 Born in Tokyo
2013 Completes studies in metal carving at Graduate School of Fine Arts, Tokyo University of the Arts
2014 Adjunct education and research assistant in metal carving, Department of Crafts, Tokyo University of the Arts (until 2017)

主な個展

2012 「吉田泰一郎展—金属の膚—」(gallery元町／神奈川)
2018 「吉田泰一郎—唸り—」(gallery小暮／東京)

主なグループ展

2009 「第10回全日本金銀創作展」(GINZA TANAKA HALL／東京)
2010 「第26回公募2010日本ジュエリーアート展」(上野の森美術館／東京ほか)
2014 「螺旋人間」(LOWER AKIHABARA.／東京)
2016 「彫金戦攻展」(日本橋三越本館6階美術特選画廊／東京)
2018 「日本當代雕塑展」(多納藝術／台湾)
2020 「ブレイク前夜展」(GINZA SIX Artglorieux／東京)
「伽—山本タカト×吉田泰一郎—」(gallery小暮／東京)
「ブレイク前夜 in 代官山ヒルサイドテラス 時代を突っ走れ!」展(ヒルサイドフォーラム／東京)
「artTNZ」(TERRADA ART COMPLEX II／東京)
「試展」(金澤水銀窟／石川)
「artKYOTO2020」(二条城／京都)
2021 「アートフェア東京 2021」(東京国際フォーラム gallery小暮ブース)['22]
「妖—AYAKASHI」展(Bunkamura Gallery／東京)
「アート大阪 2021」(大阪市中央公会堂)
「始点と交点—工芸のモーメント—」(旧平櫛田中邸／東京)
「KOGEI Art Fair Kanazawa」(ハイアットセントリック金沢／石川)
「ULTRA OBJECT vol.3」(gallery小暮／東京)
2023 「超絶技巧、未来へ! 明治工芸とそのDNA」(岐阜県現代陶芸美術館ほか)

主な受賞歴

2009 「第10回全日本金銀創作展」東京都中小企業団体中央会会長賞
2012 安宅賞
2013 原田賞
台東区長奨励賞

書籍

- 芸術新聞社監修『現代彫刻アンソロジー』、芸術新聞社、2020年

定期刊行物

- 「世界を「アッ」と言わせる、手わざとカタチ!!「超・立体」アートとしての最新工芸」『月刊美術』No.497、サン・アート、2017年2月号
- 山下裕二「山下裕二の今月の隠し球Vol.168 吉田泰一郎 間に合わなかった超絶技巧作家(上)」『美術の窓』No.423・424、生活の友社、2018年12月・19年1月号 *Vol.169(下)
- 「新時代の技巧 エナジーは細部に宿る」『月刊アートコレクターズ』No.129、生活の友社、2019年12月号
- 「「いきもの」造形最前線」『炎芸術』No.146、阿部出版、2021年5月号
- 「そばで愛でたい 立体アート」『月刊アートコレクターズ』No.150、生活の友社、2021年9月号
- 「吉田泰一郎」『ExtrART』No.31、アトリエサード、2021年12月号

作品リスト
List of Works

1 すがた―迫る！
Appearance—Approach!

1-1 [p.031]
今井完眞 | Imai Sadamasa
フシギバナ | Venusaur
陶器、手びねり、上絵付 |
stoneware, hand building, overglaze enamels
h50 70×53

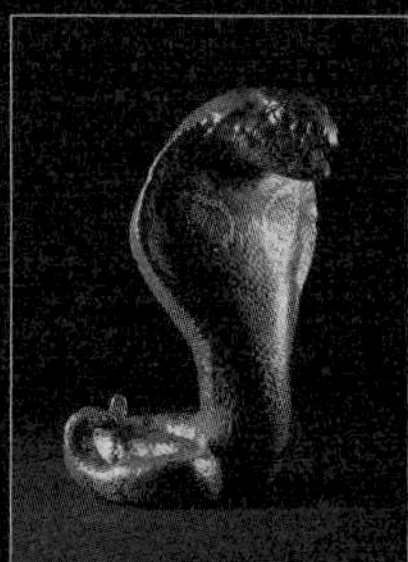

1-2 [p.030]
今井完眞 | Imai Sadamasa
アーボック | Arbok
陶器、手びねり、上絵付 |
stoneware, hand building, overglaze enamels
h44.6 36×33

1-3 [p.029]
今井完眞 | Imai Sadamasa
キングラー | Kingler
陶器、手びねり、上絵付 |
stoneware, hand building, overglaze enamels
h35.5 33.6×31

1-4 [p.028：右 | right]
今井完眞 | Imai Sadamasa
ゼニガメ | Squirtle
陶器、手びねり、上絵付 |
stoneware, hand building, overglaze enamels
h25 25.6×20

1-5 [p.028：左 | left]
今井完眞 | Imai Sadamasa
コイキング | Magikarp
陶器、手びねり、上絵付 |
stoneware, hand building, overglaze enamels
h24 32.4×20.6

2-1 [p.034]
葉山有樹 | Hayama Yuki
森羅万象ポケモン壷 |
Vase with Pokémon of the Universe
磁器、染付、上絵付 |
porcelain, underglaze enamels, overglaze enamels
h35.8 φ35.3

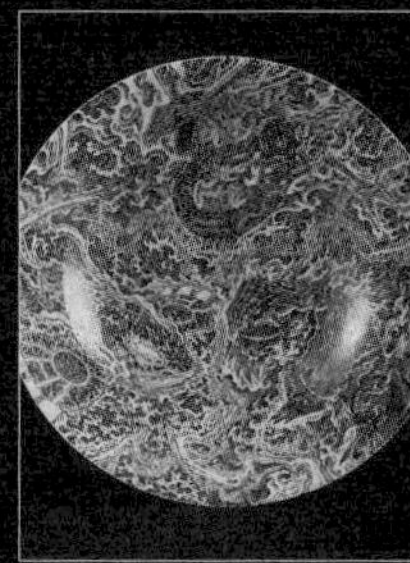

2-2 [p.035]
葉山有樹 | Hayama Yuki
超古代ポケモン玉盌 |
Beautiful Bowl with the Super-Ancient Pokémon
磁器、染付 |
porcelain, underglaze enamels
h11 φ46

3-1 [p.023]
福田亨 | Fukuda Toru
飛昇 | Flying
木（ピンクアイボリー、モチノキ、ニガキ、イエローハート、ホオノキ、イスノキ、神代ナラ、コクタン、トチ、ブラックチェリー、シナノキ、ヤマザクラ、ハゼノキ、パロサント、ヤナギ[緑青腐れ]、クスノキ）、木象嵌、指物 |
wood (pink ivory, ilex integra, picrasma quassioides, amarello, Japanese white bark magnolia, *isu* tree, Japanese oak, ebony, Japanese horse-chestnut, black cherry, Japanese torreya, jamasakura, wax tree, palo santo, willow [blued by hlorosplenium aeruginosum], camphor tree), inlay, joining
h70 42.5×30.3

凡例 | Notes
- 作品の制作年はCat.no.9,14-3–14-5,14-7,14-8,14-11,16-1,16-2（2023年）を除き2022年
- 作品はすべて個人蔵
- 表記は以下のとおり
  作品番号[掲載ページ]
  作家名
  作品名
  素材技法
  寸法（センチメートル 高さ、長辺×短辺／高さ、径／着物は丈×幅）
- All works produced in 2022 except for Cat.no.9,14-3–14-5,14-7,14-8,14-11,16-1,16-2(2023).
- All works featured from the private collection.
- On each works of information is giving in the following order:
  Catalogue no. [Page]
  Name of Artist
  Title
  Material and technique
  Dimensions (cm, height, long×short sides / height, diameter / length×width for kimonos)

3-2 [p.024]
福田亨 | Fukuda Toru
雨あがり | After Rain
木(ハゼノキ、ピンクアイボリー、神代ナラ、センノキ[緑青腐れ]、モチノキ、コクタン、ホオノキ、ブラックウォールナット、神代ニレ)、木象嵌、指物 |
wood (wax tree, pink ivory, Japanese oak, kalopanax septemlobus [blued by hlorosplenium aeruginosum], ilex integra, ebony, Japanese white bark magnolia, black walnut, elms), inlay, joining
h16 33×18

3-3 [p.025]
福田亨 | Fukuda Toru
Floor | Floor
木(ピンクアイボリー、コクタン、アマレロ、パープルハート、モチノキ、ミズナラ、パロサント、メープル)、木象嵌、指物、寄木 |
wood (pink ivory, ebony, amarello, purpleheart, ilex integra, quercus crispula, palo santo, maple), inlay, joining, marquetry
h10.3 26.8×20.4

4-1 [p.019]
満田晴穂 | Mitsuta Haruo
自在コクーン・スピアー |
Articulated Kakuna/Beedrill
真鍮、銀、銅、赤銅、彫金、打出し、象嵌、色上げ |
brass, silver, copper, *shakudo* (copper alloy with gold), engraving, hammering, inlay, patination
h11 7×7

4-2 [p.018]
満田晴穂 | Mitsuta Haruo
自在トランセル・バタフリー |
Articulated Metapod/Butterfree
銅、銀、赤銅、彫金、打出し、象嵌、色上げ |
copper, silver, *shakudo* (copper alloy with gold), engraving, hammering, inlay, patination
h13 9×7

4-3 [pp.016–017]
満田晴穂 | Mitsuta Haruo
自在ギャラドス |
Articulated Gyarados
銅、銀、真鍮、彫金、打出し、象嵌、色上げ |
copper, silver, brass, engraving, hammering, inlay, patination
h25 80×20

5-1 [p.011 : 左 | left]
吉田泰一郎 | Yoshida Taiichiro
イーブイ | Eevee
銅、銀鍍金、彫金、打出し、色上げ、七宝 |
copper, silver gilding, engraving, hammering, patination, cloisonné
h35 39×22

5-2 [pp.012–013]
吉田泰一郎 | Yoshida Taiichiro
シャワーズ | Vaporeon
銅、銀鍍金、彫金、打出し、色上げ、七宝 |
copper, silver gilding, engraving, hammering, patination, cloisonné
h75 167.5×75.3

5-3 [p.010]
吉田泰一郎 | Yoshida Taiichiro
ブースター | Flareon
銅、銀鍍金、彫金、打出し、色上げ、七宝 |
copper, silver gilding, engraving, hammering, patination, cloisonné
h102 100×56

5-4 [p.011 : 右 | right]
吉田泰一郎 | Yoshida Taiichiro
サンダース | Jolteon
銅、金鍍金、銀鍍金、彫金、打出し、色上げ、七宝 |
copper, gold gilding, silver gilding, engraving, hammering, patination, cloisonné
h62 118×45

6-1 [p.045]
池田晃将 | Ikeda Terumasa
未知文黒御影茶器 |
Tea caddy, Unown Design, Black Granite Style
漆、鮑貝、夜光貝、白蝶貝、螺鈿 |
urushi lacquer, abalone shell, turban shell, white-lipped pearl oyster, *raden* inlay
h9.1 6.2×5.1

6-2 [p.044]
池田晃将 | Ikeda Terumasa
百千光絵素飾箱「壱伍零」 |
Ornamental Box, "Mewtwo," Luminous Design, *Raden* Inlay
漆、夜光貝、螺鈿、蒔絵 |
urushi lacquer, turban shell, *raden* inlay, *maki-e*
h3 8.1×6.6

6-3 [p.047]
池田晃将 | Ikeda Terumasa
電線光環中次 |
Tea Caddy, Electric Exchange Design
漆、夜光貝、鮑貝、白蝶貝、螺鈿 |
urushi lacquer, turban shell, abalone shell, white-lipped pearl oyster, *raden* inlay
h8.6 6.2×5.4

6-4 [p.046]
池田晃将 | Ikeda Terumasa
電光投擲捕獲箱 | Poké Ball Box
漆、鮑貝、黒蝶貝、夜光貝、螺鈿、蒔絵 |
urushi lacquer, abalone shell, black-lipped pearl oyster, turban shell, *raden* inlay, *maki-e*
h4.1 4.1×4.1

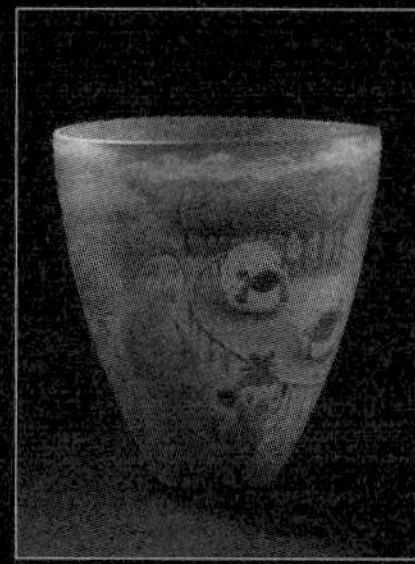

7-1 [p.056]
池本一三 | Ikemoto Kazumi
冒険のはじまり | Adventure Begins
ガラス、キャスト、エナメル吹付 |
glass, casting, enamel spraying
h50 45×45

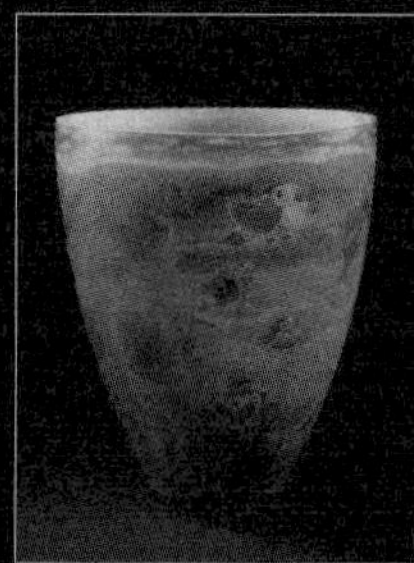

7-2 [p.057]
池本一三 | Ikemoto Kazumi
湖のほとりで | By the Lake
ガラス、キャスト、エナメル吹付 |
glass, casting, enamel spraying
h50 45×45

7-3 [p.058]
池本一三 | Ikemoto Kazumi
殿堂入り | Hall of Fame
ガラス、キャスト、エナメル吹付 |
glass, casting, enamel spraying
h50 45×45

8-1 [p.075]
城間栄市 | Shiroma Eiichi
琉球紅型着物「島ツナギ」 |
Kimono "Island to Island," Ryukyu *Bingata*
絹、型染 | silk, stencil dyeing
178×138

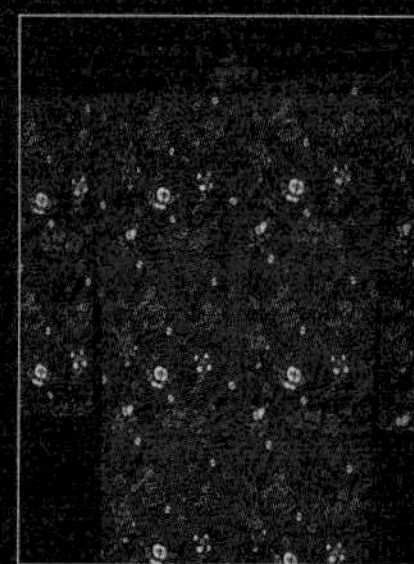

8-2 [p.076]
城間栄市 | Shiroma Eiichi
琉球藍型着物「島ツナギ」 |
Kimono "Island to Island," Ryukyu *Egata*
絹、型染、浸染 |
silk, stencil dyeing, dip-dyeing
178×138

9 [pp.080–081]
須藤玲子 | Sudo Reiko
ピカチュウの森 |
Pikachu's Adventures in a Forest
インスタレーション | Installation
綿、ニードルレース |
cotton, needle lace (machine made)

10 [p.041]
田中信行｜Tanaka Nobuyuki
無題｜Untitled
漆、乾漆、髹漆｜
urushi lacquer, *kanshitsu*, *kyushitsu* (*urushi* lacquering)
h207 106×70

11 [p.068–071]
坪島悠貴｜Tsuboshima Yuki
可変金物 ココガラ/アーマーガア｜
Transformable Ornament, Rookidee/Corviknight
銀、リン青銅、ロストワックス、電着塗装｜
silver, phosphor bronze, lost-wax casting, electrodeposition coating
ココガラ：h4.9 7.6×6.9
アーマーガア：h6.3 12×7.2

12 [p.050]
新實広記｜Niimi Hiroki
Vessel –TSURARA–｜
Vessel –TSURARA–
インスタレーション｜Installation
ガラス、キャスト、研磨｜
glass, casting, polishing

13 [p.063]
林茂樹｜Hayashi Shigeki
月光 Pokémon Edition｜
"Moonlight" Pokémon Edition
磁器、鋳込み、上絵付｜
porcelain, slip casting, overglaze enamels
h100 38×36

14-1 [p.104]
植葉香澄｜Ueba Kasumi
光火彩文グラードン｜
Groudon with Flash and Flame Pattern
陶器、手びねり、上絵付｜
stoneware, hand building, overglaze enamels
h70 60×40

14-2 [p.107]
植葉香澄｜Ueba Kasumi
羊歯唐草文シェイミ｜
Shaymin with Fern Arabesque Pattern
陶器、手びねり、上絵付｜
stoneware, hand building, overglaze enamels
h30 35×30

14-3
植葉香澄｜Ueba Kasumi
羊歯唐草文シェイミ茶碗｜
Shaymin Teabowl with Fern Arabesque Pattern
陶器、手びねり、上絵付｜
stoneware, hand building, overglaze enamels
h11 16×16

14-4
植葉香澄｜Ueba Kasumi
唐草文サルノリ｜
Grookey with Arabesque Pattern
陶器、手びねり、上絵付｜
stoneware, hand building, overglaze enamels
h65 63×46

14-5
植葉香澄｜Ueba Kasumi
唐草文サルノリポートレイト｜
Grookey Portrait with Arabesque Pattern
陶器、手びねり、上絵付｜
stoneware, hand building, overglaze enamels
h28 26×19

14-6 [p.106：中｜middle]
植葉香澄｜Ueba Kasumi
唐草文サルノリ茶碗｜
Grookey Teabowl with Arabesque Pattern
陶器、手びねり、上絵付｜
stoneware, hand building, overglaze enamels
h11 16×16

14-7
植葉香澄｜Ueba Kasumi
火炎文ヒバニー｜
Scorbunny with Flame Pattern
陶器、手びねり、上絵付｜
stoneware, hand building, overglaze enamels
h61 41×37

14-8
植葉香澄｜Ueba Kasumi
火炎文ヒバニーポートレイト｜
Scorbunny Portrait with Flame Pattern
陶器、手びねり、上絵付｜
stoneware, hand building, overglaze enamels
h35 28×14

14-9 [p.106：上 | top]
植葉香澄 | Ueba Kasumi
火炎文ヒバニー茶碗 |
Scorbunny Teabowl with Flame Pattern
陶器、手びねり、上絵付 |
stoneware, hand building, overglaze enamels
h11 16×16

14-10 [p.105]
植葉香澄 | Ueba Kasumi
水文メッソン |
Sobble with Water Pattern
陶器、手びねり、上絵付 |
stoneware, hand building, overglaze enamels
h70 60×40

14-11
植葉香澄 | Ueba Kasumi
水文メッソンポートレイト |
Sobble Portrait with Water Pattern
陶器、手びねり、上絵付 |
stoneware, hand building, overglaze enamels
h41 28×15

14-12 [p.106：下 | bottom]
植葉香澄 | Ueba Kasumi
水文メッソン茶碗 |
Sobble Teabowl with Water Pattern
陶器、手びねり、上絵付 |
stoneware, hand building, overglaze enamels
h11 16×16

15-1 [p.089：下 | bottom]
桂盛仁 | Katsura Morihito
帯留 ブラッキー「立ち姿」 |
Sash Clasp in Umbreon Shape, “Standing”
赤銅、金、銀、銅、彫金、打出し、象嵌、色上げ |
shakudo (copper alloy with gold), gold, silver, copper, engraving, hammering, inlay, patination
h1.5 5×4.5

15-2 [p.089：上 | top]
桂盛仁 | Katsura Morihito
帯留 ブラッキー「威嚇」 |
Sash Clasp in Umbreon Shape, “Intimidating”
赤銅、金、銀、銅、彫金、打出し、象嵌、色上げ |
shakudo (copper alloy with gold), gold, silver, copper, engraving, hammering, inlay, patination
h1.5 6.5×4

15-3 [p.089：中 | middle]
桂盛仁 | Katsura Morihito
ブローチ ブラッキー「眠り」 |
Brooch in Umbreon Shape, “Sleep”
赤銅、金、銀、銅、彫金、打出し、象嵌、色上げ |
shakudo (copper alloy with gold), gold, silver, copper, engraving, hammering, inlay, patination
h1.5 6×3.5

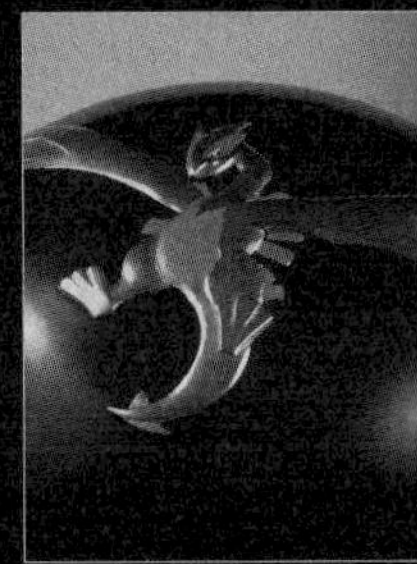

15-4 [p.087]
桂盛仁 | Katsura Morihito
香合 ルギア |
Incense Container, Lugia Design
唐金、銀、象嵌、彫金 |
bronze, silver, inlay, engraving
h5.4 φ9.6

15-5 [p.086]
桂盛仁 | Katsura Morihito
香合 ホウオウ |
Incense Container, Ho-Oh Design
唐金、金、象嵌、彫金 |
bronze, gold, inlay, engraving
h5.4 φ9.6

16-1 [pp.098–099]
桑田卓郎 | Kuwata Takuro
カップ（ピカチュウ） | Cups (Pikachu)
インスタレーション | Installation
磁器、釉薬、動力成形、金白銀彩、転写 |
porcelain, glaze, machine molding, overglaze gold and platinum, transfer printing

16-2
桑田卓郎｜Kuwata Takuro
ボウル（ピカチュウ）｜Bowls (Pikachu)
インスタレーション｜Installation
陶器、釉薬、轆轤成形、金白銀彩、転写｜stoneware, glaze, throwing, overglaze gold and platinum, transfer printing

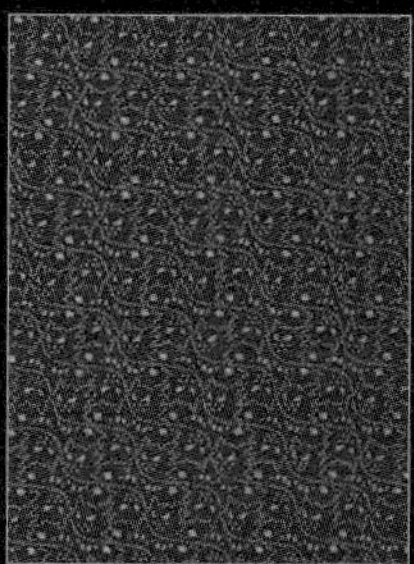

17-1 [p.123]
小宮康義｜Komiya Yasuyoshi
江戸小紋 着尺「ゲンガー・ゴースト」｜Kimono Cloth, Edo *Komon*, "Gengar and Haunter"
絹、型染｜silk, stencil dyeing
1300×37

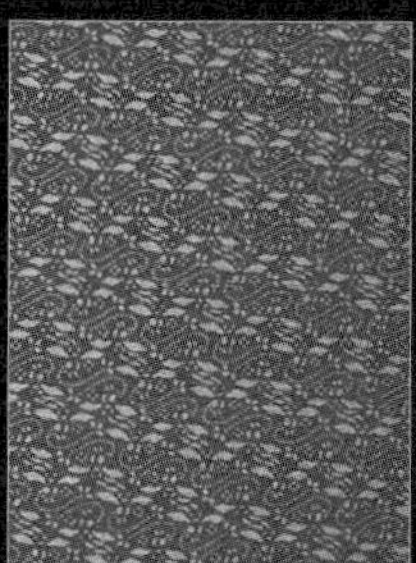

17-2 [p.121]
小宮康義｜Komiya Yasuyoshi
江戸小紋 着尺「フライゴン」｜Kimono Cloth, Edo *Komon*, "Flygon"
絹、型染｜silk, stencil dyeing
1300×37

17-3 [p.120]
小宮康義｜Komiya Yasuyoshi
江戸小紋 着尺「タマゲタケ・モロバレル」｜Kimono Cloth, Edo *Komon*, "Foongus and Amoonguss"
絹、型染｜silk, stencil dyeing
1300×37

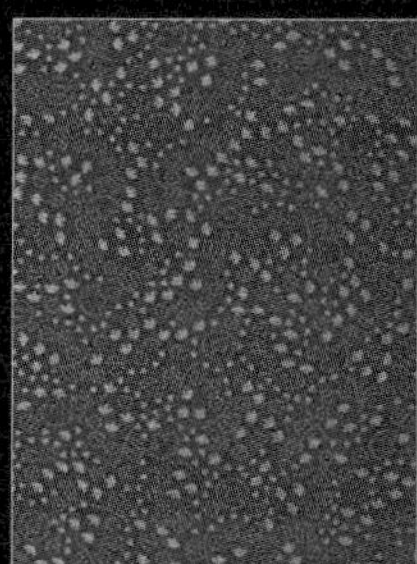

17-4 [p.122]
小宮康義｜Komiya Yasuyoshi
江戸小紋 着尺「ガラルマッギョ」｜Kimono Cloth, Edo *Komon*, "Galarian Stunfisk"
絹、型染｜silk, stencil dyeing
1300×37

17-5
小宮康義｜Komiya Yasuyoshi
江戸小紋 着物「ゲンガー・ゴースト」｜Kimono, Edo *Komon*, "Gengar and Haunter"
絹、型染｜silk, stencil dyeing
159×136

18-1 [p.093]
田口義明｜Taguchi Yoshiaki
乾漆蒔絵螺鈿蓋物「遊」｜Lidded Jar, "Play," *Kanshitsu*, *Maki-e* and *Raden* Inlay
漆、白蝶貝、乾漆、蒔絵、螺鈿｜*urushi* lacquer, white-lipped pearl oyster, *kanshitsu*, *maki-e*, *raden* inlay
h19 φ21.7

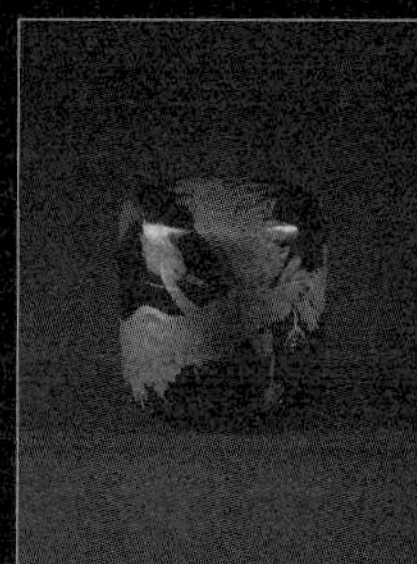

18-2 [p.094]
田口義明｜Taguchi Yoshiaki
蒔絵棗「春を呼ぶ」｜Tea Caddy, "Call Spring," *Maki-e*
漆、蒔絵｜*urushi* lacquer, *maki-e*
h8.1 φ7.2

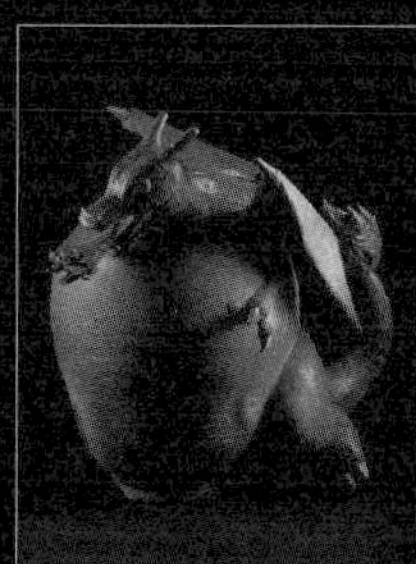

19-1 [p.110]
桝本佳子｜Masumoto Keiko
リザードン／信楽壷｜Charizard/Shigaraki Jar
陶器、轆轤成形、手びねり｜stoneware, throwing, hand building
h82 80×62

19-2 [p.112：右｜right]
桝本佳子｜Masumoto Keiko
信楽壷／キュウコン｜Shigaraki Jar/Ninetales
陶器、轆轤成形、手びねり、化粧掛け、上絵付｜stoneware, throwing, hand building, engobe, overglaze enamels
h60 40×40

19-3 [p.112：左｜left]
桝本佳子｜Masumoto Keiko
ロコン／信楽壷｜Vulpix/Shigaraki Jar
陶器、轆轤成形、手びねり｜stoneware, throwing, hand building
h41 43×30

19-4
桝本佳子｜Masumoto Keiko
ヒトカゲ／信楽壷｜Charmander/Shigaraki Jar
陶器、轆轤成形、手びねり｜stoneware, throwing, hand building
h48 40×33

19-5 [p.111]
桝本佳子 | Masumoto Keiko
信楽壷／ファイヤー |
Shigaraki Jar/Moltres
陶器、轆轤成形、手びねり、化粧掛け、上絵付 |
stoneware, throwing, hand building, engobe, overglaze enamels
h40 45×45

19-6 [p.113：上 | top]
桝本佳子 | Masumoto Keiko
キャモメ／染付皿 |
Wingull/Underglazed Plate
半磁器、轆轤成形、手びねり、染付、上絵付 |
semi-porcelain, throwing, hand building, underglaze enamels, overglaze enamels
h18 56×42

19-7
桝本佳子 | Masumoto Keiko
マンタイン／染付皿 |
Mantine/Underglazed Plate
半磁器、轆轤成形、手びねり、染付 |
semi-porcelain, throwing, hand building, underglaze enamels
h24 68×65

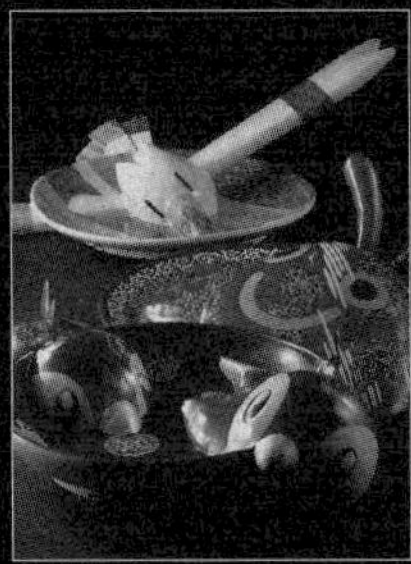

19-8 [p.113：中 | middle]
桝本佳子 | Masumoto Keiko
タマンタ／染付皿 |
Mantyke/Underglazed Plate
半磁器、轆轤成形、手びねり、染付 |
semi-porcelain, throwing, hand building, underglaze enamels
h18 46×40

19-9 [p.113：下 | bottom]
桝本佳子 | Masumoto Keiko
ポッチャマ／染付皿 |
Piplup/Underglazed Plate
半磁器、轆轤成形、手びねり、染付、上絵付 |
semi-porcelain, throwing, hand building, underglaze enamels, overglaze enamels
h12 55×43

19-10
桝本佳子 | Masumoto Keiko
タマゴ／壷 | Egg/Jar
陶器（紫香楽陶土）、轆轤成形、手びねり、上絵付 |
stoneware (*shigaraki* clay), throwing, hand building, overglaze enamels
h21 13×12

19-11
桝本佳子 | Masumoto Keiko
マホミル／壷 | Milcery/Jar
半磁器、轆轤成形、手びねり、上絵付 |
semi-porcelain, throwing, hand building, overglaze enamels
h18 22×15

19-12
桝本佳子 | Masumoto Keiko
タネボー／壷 | Seedot/Jar
陶器（黒御影土）、轆轤成形、手びねり、上絵付 |
stoneware (kuromikage clay), throwing, hand building, overglaze enamels
h17 20×14

19-13
桝本佳子 | Masumoto Keiko
ヌメラ／壷 | Goomy/Jar
半磁器、轆轤成形、手びねり、上絵付 |
semi-porcelain, throwing, hand building, overglaze enamels
h30 20×18

20-1 [p.117]
水橋さおり | Mizuhashi Saori
友禅訪問着「群」|
Kimono, "Herd," *Yuzen* Dyeing
絹、友禅 | silk, *yuzen* dyeing
180×140

20-2 [p.116]
水橋さおり | Mizuhashi Saori
友禅帯「閃光」|
Sash, "Flash," *Yuzen* Dyeing
絹、友禅 | silk, *yuzen* dyeing
500×35

写真撮影
斎城卓：pp.10–13, 16–19, 22–25, 28–31, 34–35, 38, 40–41, 44–47, 50–53, 56–59, 62–65, 68–71, 74–77, 86–89, 92–95, 98–101, 104–107, 110–113, 116–117, 120–123, 165
林雅之：pp.80–82, 84

写真提供
池本一三
池田晃将
今井完眞
植葉香澄
小宮康義
田口義明
田中信行
坪島悠貴
新實広記
林茂樹
福田亨
桝本佳子
水橋さおり
満田晴穂
吉田泰一郎
株式会社ポケモン

取材協力
株式会社エンラージ

協力
株式会社アートジャパン・靖山画廊
Gallery花影抄／根津の根付屋

Photo Credit
Saiki Taku: pp.10–13, 16–19, 22–25, 28–31, 34–35, 38, 40–41, 44–47, 50–53, 56–59, 62–65, 68–71, 74–77, 86–89, 92–95, 98–101, 104–107, 110–113, 116–117, 120–123, 165
Hayashi Masayuki: pp.80–82, 84

Photo Courtesy
Ikemoto Kazumi
Ikeda Terumasa
Imai Sadamasa
Ueba Kasumi
Komiya Yasuyoshi
Taguchi Yoshiaki
Tanaka Nobuyuki
Tsuboshima Yuki
Niimi Hiroki
Hayashi Shigeki
Fukuda Toru
Masumoto Keiko
Mizuhashi Saori
Mitsuta Haruo
Yoshida Taiichiro
The Pokémon Company

Cooperation with Coverage
Enlarge Co., Ltd.

Cooperation
Art Japan Co.,Ltd / SEIZAN GALLERY
Gallery Hanakagesho Nezu no Netsukeya

開催概要

ポケモン×工芸展
美とわざの大発見

2023年3月21日–6月11日
国立工芸館
主催：国立工芸館、NHKエンタープライズ中部、
読売新聞北陸支社
特別協力：株式会社ポケモン
制作協力：NHKプロモーション
後援：石川県、金沢市、北國新聞社、テレビ金沢

POKÉMON × KOGEI
Playful Encounters of Pokémon and Japanese Craft

March 21–June 11, 2023
National Crafts Museum
Organizer: National Crafts Musem,
NHK ENTERPRISES INC. Nagoya Branch Office,
The Yomiuri Shimbun Hokuriku Branch Office
Special cooperation: The Pokémon Company
Produced: NHK Promotions Inc.
Supported: Ishikawa Prefecture, Kanazawa City,
THE HOKKOKU SHIMBUN,
Television Kanazawa Corporation

ポケモン×工芸
美とわざの大発見

監修
国立工芸館

テキスト
唐澤昌宏(国立工芸館)
今井陽子(国立工芸館)

編集
国立工芸館
唐澤昌宏、岩井美恵子、今井陽子、横川悠子、日南日和
—
黒川典是

アートディレクション
中野豪雄(中野デザイン事務所)
デザイン
西垣由紀子(中野デザイン事務所)

翻訳
中野勉:pp.2–3, 7
クリストファー・スティヴンズ:pp.14–15, 26–27, 36–37, 42–43, 48–49, 54–55, 78–79, 82–83, 108–109, 114–115
ルーシー・S・マクレリー:pp.20–21, 32–33, 60–61, 66–67, 72–73, 90–91, 96–97, 102–103, 118–119, 124–125

制作協力
株式会社NHKプロモーション

特別協力
株式会社ポケモン
The Pokémon Company International

発行日
2023年4月6日 初版第1刷発行
2024年12月25日 初版第6刷発行

発行者
大河内雅彦
発行所
株式会社東京美術
〒170-0011 東京都豊島区池袋本町3-31-15
電話 03(5391)9031
FAX 03(3982)3295
https: //www.tokyo-bijutsu.co.jp

印刷
株式会社アイワード

POKÉMON × KOGEI
Playful Encounters of Pokémon and Japanese Craft

Supervisor
National Crafts Museum

Text
Karasawa Masahiro (National Crafts Museum)
Imai Yoko (National Crafts Museum)

Editor
National Crafts Museum
Karasawa Masahiro, Iwai Mieko, Imai Yoko, Yokogawa Yuko, Himinami Hiyori
—
Kurokawa Noriyuki

Art Director
Nakano Takeo (Nakano Design Office)
Designer
Nishigaki Yukiko (Nakano Design Office)

Translator
Nakano Tsutomu: pp.2–3, 7
Christopher Stephens: pp.14–15, 26–27, 36–37, 42–43, 48–49, 54–55, 78–79, 82–83, 108–109, 114–115
Ruth S. McCreery: pp.20–21, 32–33, 60–61, 66–67, 72–73, 90–91, 96–97, 102–103, 118–119, 124–125

Production Cooperation
NHK Promotions Inc.

Special Cooperation
The Pokémon Company
The Pokémon Company International

Edition
April 6, 2023 (First)
December 25, 2024 (Sixth)

Publisher
Ohkohchi Masahiko
Published by
TOKYO BIJUTSU Co., Ltd.
3-31-15 Ikebukuro-honcho, Toshima-ku, Tokyo
170-0011, JAPAN
tel: +81-3-5391-9031 fax: +81-3-3982-3295
https: //www.tokyo-bijutsu.co.jp

Printed by
iWORD Co., Ltd.

ISBN978-4-8087-1268-6 C0072